MW01610251

IGNITE THE SPARK

IGNITE THE SPARK

52 Creative Ways to
Boost Productivity

JUDI MOREO
FIONA CARMICHAEL

PENGUIN BOOKS

PENGUIN BOOKS

Published by the Penguin Group
80 Strand, London WC2R 0RL, England
Penguin Putnam Inc, 375 Hudson Street, New York, New York 10014, USA
Penguin Books Australia Ltd, 250 Camberwell Road, Camberwell,
Victoria 3124, Australia
Penguin Books Canada Ltd, 10 Alcorn Avenue, Toronto, Ontario,
Canada M4V 3B2
Penguin Books (NZ) Ltd, Cnr Rosedale and Airborne Roads, Albany,
Auckland, New Zealand
Penguin Books India (P) Ltd, 11 Community Centre, Panchsheel Park,
New Delhi – 110 017, India
Penguin Books (South Africa) (Pty) Ltd, 24 Sturdee Avenue, Rosebank,
Johannesburg 2196, South Africa

Penguin Books (South Africa) (Pty) Ltd, Registered Offices:
Second Floor, 90 Rivonia Road, Sandton 2196, South Africa

First published by National Press Publications, Inc 2002
Published by Penguin Books (South Africa) (Pty) Ltd 2003

Copyright © Judi Moreo/Fiona Carmichael 2002
All rights reserved
The moral right of the authors has been asserted

ISBN 0 143 02433 7

Typeset by Mckore Graphics, Cape Town
Cover design: African Icons
Printed and bound by Formeset Printers, Cape Town

Except in the United States of America, this book is sold subject to the condition that
it shall not, by way of trade or otherwise, be lent, resold, hired out or otherwise cir-
culated without the publisher's prior consent in any form of binding or cover other
than that in which it is published and without a similar condition including this condition being imposed on the subsequent purchaser.

CONTENTS

INTRODUCTION

Ignite The Spark: 52 Creative Ways to Boost Productivity provides a comprehensive set of tools and techniques that will give you the ability to capture the creativity of your team members. Unleashing this kind of mental energy is, of course, the challenge of today's managers and team leaders. This book will show you how! In addition, you will learn how to successfully lead your team to:

- Boost creativity.
- Improve teamwork.
- Increase productivity.
- Reduce problems.
- Make decisions.
- Improve thinking.

As a leader, the results you achieve depend on the following three critical factors:

1. **Getting things done through other people.** Your job is to work through the people who report to you.
2. **Needing your people more than they need you.** You get results through them. You can't do everything yourself. Your time is a limited resource.
3. **Getting paid for what your people do.** Your ability to harness the creativity of the people on your team is instrumental in helping you achieve results.

The 21st century demands 21st-century thinking! In a world of accelerating change, the most effective approach will be one of offence rather than defence. Competitors are swiftly managing to copy the winning ways of your organisation. To survive this increasingly unpredictable and competitive environment, you need to find ways to mobilise and pull together the brainpower of all your employees. Innovation has become more important than ever before, and your organisation's future will depend on your ability to unleash creativity in the workplace.

We are in the digital age. Speed drives the 21st-century economy, and change is occurring at an unprecedented pace. This is an age of intensified global interdependence. As the world speeds up and business becomes more intense, managing the impact that this ongoing change has on your people will be your most serious challenge. A mindset of reactivity and control will most definitely fail. The more rapid the change, the more radical the shift and the more likely that your usual approaches will lose their power.

As the powerful forces of change continue at breakneck speed, there is a lot more evidence available proving that slow-changing organisations are headed for trouble. High-velocity change is here to stay. Smart organisations will create their own change. Your challenge will be to stimulate new thinking.

'Discovery consists of looking at the same thing as everyone else and thinking something different.'
Albert Szent-Gyorgyi

In order to succeed, you must find and utilise the creativity in your organisation. Creativity is not a fad. It's not something that is here today and will be replaced by a new concept tomorrow. The entire organisation should become obsessed with looking for and finding an even better way to capture its creative power. Just imagine the creative power that comes when part of everyone's job is to find new ways of doing things, when team members are constantly on the lookout for how to do their jobs better and are searching for new solutions. An organisation that is geared towards maximising the talent, skills and abilities of its people by tapping into the creativity of its work force is sure to thrive.

Dr Jim Botkin, author of *Smart Business*, says, 'Failure to innovate means death for any organisation in a world that increasingly measures by Internet years.' (An Internet year is equivalent to three calendar months.) Throughout history, failure to innovate caused companies to fail. One example is Tudor Ice Company. Back in 1859, business was booming. The owners focused on doing what they had always done: harvesting natural ice. Tudor had a monopoly on the ice market and grew steadily for 25 years. But the times were changing. The patent for machine-made ice was registered in the mid-1800s, and a solid newcomer, the refrigerator, was gaining in popularity. By the early 1900s, refrigerators were in, iceboxes were out and the Tudor Ice Company was bankrupt.

Other examples include America's first textile mill as well as one of the most successful computer manufacturers, both of which succumbed to the same fate. The Lowell, Massachusetts, mill went out of business when it failed to adapt to new weaving machinery and to find a way to compete with cheap labour. The empty brick factory buildings in many New England towns are stark reminders. Digital Equipment Company failed to recognise the value of the personal computer and the importance of compatibility. Compaq understood both and eventually bought out Digital. There are hundreds of companies with the same fate.

If you don't act, then you will be acted upon. The only way to succeed is to continuously find ways to improve. You can do that when innovation and creativity thrive in your organisation. As Rosabeth Moss Kanter so aptly states, 'To stay ahead you must have your next idea waiting in the wings.'

Organisations that think improvement means doing the same old things, only better, will be eliminated by natural selection. Business today requires continuous renewal, and continuous renewal means anticipating change, adapting appropriately and committing to innovation. Organisations will be able to achieve this renewal by nurturing and encouraging their employees to be more knowledgeable and more creative.

HOW TO GET THE MOST OUT OF THIS BOOK

Conventional thinking can't keep up with exceptional change. This book is meant to crank up your thinking and the thinking of your team, as well as to challenge you to go beyond the boundaries of the ways you have always done things. Look at doing things from fresh angles – operate from a different perspective to break the pattern of your thinking that causes immobilisation and stifles creativity – so that you are more solution-oriented and less problem-focused.

In most organisations, the capabilities of employees drive the success of the business. To be a high-performance player in today's demanding marketplace, your organisation must focus on how fast your team members increase their capabilities. *Ignite The Spark* provides a comprehensive set of tools and techniques that will give you the ability to nurture and capture the creativity of your team. Unleashing that kind of mental energy is the challenge for today's managers and team leaders. This book shows you how by providing you with 52 mind workouts, so that you can implement one idea each week for one year. If you stick with the concept of using one idea each week, you will boost the creativity in your organisation and learn bold, new ways to successfully lead your team to:
- Think smart.
- Improve teamwork.
- Increase productivity.

- Solve problems.
- Improve old ways of doing business.
- Make decisions.
- Make initiatives happen.
- Brainstorm ideas.
- Create new products.

The overall format of this book is solution-oriented. It has been purposely designed for quick reference and easy reading. The application of many of the notions, tools and techniques is intended to give you a competitive edge. Utilising the information and techniques in this book will enable you to dramatically improve performance and productivity levels. Over time, this will ultimately lead to huge payoffs and have a significant impact on results.

WHAT TO EXPECT

The basic premise of this book is to get your team members to recognise how they can be creative. Many of us sense that our team members are more creative, but we are unable to effectively tap into that creativity. Many people are creatively blocked. This book provides simple and effective breakthrough techniques that you can use to ignite the spark of creativity in your team members. You will be creating pathways through which their creative forces can operate. When you are able to loosen up the thinking abilities of your team and when preconceived notions or conclusions no longer block ideas, you will know you are succeeding. Here's an example.

The leg of a low chair breaks and two men in a small cabin seek to prop it up immediately. Both of them look for a stick the right size, but there is nothing around except for a hammer.

One man sees the hammer and forgets it because, in his mind, a hammer is a tool for hammering and nothing else. The other man looks with an open, creative attitude. He picks up the hammer, which is exactly the right length, and uses it as a chair leg. He bypassed the mental block that limited the uses of the hammer!

Building a creative and innovative organisation is no easy feat. That is why we have based the teachings of this book on two elements.

1. Awareness

The awareness element involves introspection, insight, realisation and the understanding of what happens in the thinking process. This includes examination, self-reflection and some serious self-evaluation as to what steps you will take to successfully use the information in this book.

2. Tools

No one has ever learned a skill just by reading about it. John Seely Brown and Paul Duguid characterise the action form of learning in this way: 'People don't become physicists by learning formulas any more than they become football players by learning plays. In learning how to be a physicist or a football player – how to act as one, talk as one, be recognised as one – it's not the explicit statements but the implicit practices that count.' Practice and application will ensure transference of the learning. For example, learning to drive a car means learning the rules of the road and having someone demonstrate how to drive a car. The learning takes place when the person gets behind the wheel. It is only when the actual experience and practice of driving the car take place that these habits will become automatic. When you're an experienced driver, you don't think of every move you have to make. It's an automatic reaction.

The same application is true with the principles of thinking. Thinking is a skill, and it is not difficult to become proficient in creative thinking. In fact, once you learn the basic principles and begin using the tools we have provided for you, your thinking abilities will drastically improve. It takes practice. Like any tools, they do not work by themselves. Just reading about them is not going to make a difference in day-to-day living. You must make them a part of your automatic thinking habits. You must practise using these tools and techniques until they become automatically ingrained, so that you are able to use them when you need them most. If you decide against taking the time to actually use them with discipline and consistency, then all we have given you are suggestions.

This book will help you tap into the skills and knowledge of the team members who are the ones handling the actual work. It will also help you to turbocharge their thinking, imagination and intelligence for maximum results. Much of their talent and competencies are underutilised. Unless your team members are encouraged to bring ideas and solutions to problems, they are not going to think creatively as readily as you would like.

As you begin using the information and tools in your everyday life, we ask you to apply these four suggestions.

The Four Suggestions
1. Put aside preconceived notions.
2. Be open to possibilities.
3. Decide to be creative.
4. Do it!

CHAPTER ONE

YOUR LEADERSHIP ROLE

Great leaders know that creativity is a key component of survival. You must demonstrate to your team members every day of every month of every year, year after year, what creativity means and how important it is to the organisation.

In a recent survey by the American Management Association, 500 CEOs were asked, 'What must one do to survive in the 21st century?' The top answer across the board was, 'Practise creativity and innovation.' Yet only 6 per cent felt their organisations were doing a great job of it. (Reported in *Psychology Today*, Sept/Oct 2000.) According to *Training & Development*, March 2001, the biggest roadblock to creativity and innovation within organisations is fear.

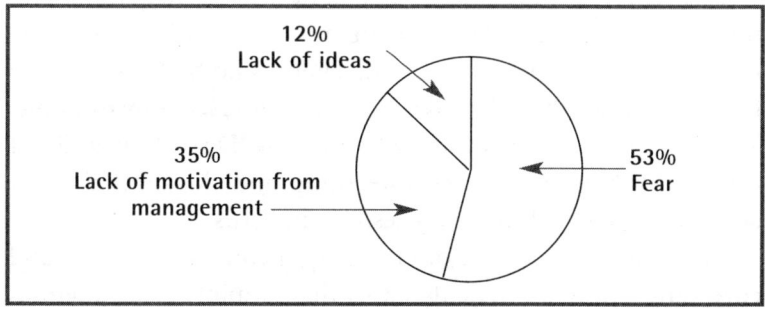

The extensive changes we are currently experiencing through-out the globe are going to demand a particular style of leadership so utterly revolutionary that it will challenge any and all existing paradigms. New thinking must become the norm in any organisation where high quality and effective leadership will be the competitive edge. It must supersede outdated and obsolete management paradigms. When there is truly effective leadership, team members are mobilised to be and do their very best. It is the catalyst for transforming the organisation and galvanising everyone towards a common purpose.

WALK THE TALK

The potential for greatness and innovation in your organisation already exists. It's up to you to recognise, retrieve and redeem this competitive capital. The answer lies in uniting your team and being able to create an environment that is conducive to creativity.

> 'As I grow older, I pay less attention to what people say. I just watch what they do.'
> Andrew Carnegie

Effective leaders know that their employees are their greatest assets. They cultivate, encourage and engage the talents and skills of these employees to be able to consistently find new and better approaches that will ultimately improve bottom-line results. They believe that understanding, participation and involvement of their team members are essential to earning respect, loyalty and commitment. There is no better way to do this than by 'walking the talk'. A true leader teaches by example. Yet there are so many leaders who practise 'Do as I say and not as I do'. When you preach one thing and do another, your adverse influence diminishes respect and trust.

To generate a culture of creativity, a company's vision and core values must be articulated so that employees see them as being high priorities. Vision stimulates and fosters creativity. This vision, along with your company's core values, must be infused into everything you say and do, so that everyone can accurately anticipate the future and avoid repeating past mistakes.

You ought to become the model of the transformation that you are envisioning. Leaders set the tone or tempo of the organisation. Powerful leadership requires that the leader model the right behaviours. Employees copy a leader's behaviour! The single most important way to ensure that your employees become the best they can be is to 'walk your talk'. If you want to be effective, don't just set values or talk values. Instead, practise and demonstrate values. Your employees make judgements about you based on what they see you do rather than what they hear you say. Actions really do speak louder than words! Make sure your actions demonstrate what you say. The failure to walk the talk results in distrust and low morale.

Mahatma Gandhi, the great Indian social reformer, was perhaps one of the greatest and most powerful leaders of all time. He personified what it means to 'walk the talk'. He believed in non-violent methods, that there must be no fighting but rather fasting and non-retaliation. His determination and willingness to set the example eventually led to his nation's independence. He defeated the British Empire with all of its military might.

This is further demonstrated by the example of a distraught Hindu man whose son had been killed by a Muslim. The Hindu man had retaliated by killing a Muslim. He approached Gandhi and asked for help, to which Gandhi answered, 'Go and find a Muslim child who has been orphaned by the riots between your two regions. Take that Muslim child into your own Hindu home and raise him as your own son, but as a Muslim.' Gandhi was a truly remarkable man who will be forever revered for his exceptional leadership.

People will believe you when you model the behaviours

'No man is fit to command another that cannot command himself.'
William Penn

3

that you want them to practise. The most natural way of influencing people is by example. If you want your employees to be more creative, then show them by being creative yourself. If you want them to be more organised, then you must be more organised. If you want them to be more enthusiastic, then enthusiasm must begin with you. If you want punctuality and you start your meetings late, that's saying it's OK not to be punctual. If you want your people to be more disciplined, then your responsibility is to begin with your own discipline.

There is hardly a company that doesn't have a communication problem of one kind or another. And yet senior managers of many organisations don't even speak to employees by saying a simple 'Good morning'. If you want the communication in your organisation to be effective, then the communication should begin with you.

Your behaviour has to correspond with whatever expectations you have of your employees. It's that simple. In his book *Sacred Cows Make The Best Burgers*, co-author Robert Kriegel tells the story of an outstanding individual, Frank Pacetta, a sales manager at Xerox, who took his district from the bottom-ranking performer to number one in his region. He says, 'I believe in the power of personal example. At the minimum, a leader has to show his troops the route of the march and the destination.' Employees who have a strong leader will look out for fresh ideas, take on new challenges and learn new things.

Suppose you announce that you are committed to customers. However, in your day-to-day behaviour, you find your customers to be bothersome and you ignore or avoid them wherever possible. Your behaviour demonstrates the opposite.

For the past 20 years, Carol Scott, managing director of Imperial Car Rental, South Africa, has spent every Tuesday between 8 am and 10 am serving customers. She knows that satisfied customers drive her business profits. This weekly habit has clearly and positively demonstrated to all of her employees as well as her customers that they are important. The result: a very successful company that has both loyal customers and employees.

If your employees see that your behaviour exemplifies a specific behaviour you want them to have, they will do as you do. The most important way to communicate your commitment is through your behaviour. All that you do sends a message: how you spend your time, the goals you set, the ways you reward performance, as well as your verbal and non-verbal communications.

We're all dealing with the same primary business issues and challenges: reducing turnover, retaining employees, attracting talent, raising performance at all levels, obtaining commitment, improving communication and accountability, overcoming roadblocks to change, doing more with fewer resources, and reducing negativity. These are the day-to-day issues that most of us have to handle. They have to be dealt with in the appropriate manner, which ultimately boils down to two words: effective leadership!

We only have to take a look at the leadership of an organisation to understand why certain companies flourish and others merely exist. Victor Goncalves, former co-founder of the very successful Villamoura restaurants, states, 'When an organisation is thriving, look at the top. It's the leader. When an organisation is stagnant, look at the top. It's the leader.' Similarly, you can walk into any business and know, within a few minutes, the kind of leader the company has at the helm by the kind of service you get. What happens at the top filters down to all employees. A leader's ability to lead is critical to the establishment and continuity of creativity, increased productivity and retention of good employees.

⚡ SELF-EVALUATION

This is the time to do a little self-evaluation. Be honest with yourself. Place a circle around the letter that indicates your answer.

		Yes	No
1.	Are you really 'walking the talk'?	Y	N
2.	Do you practise what you preach?	Y	N
3.	Are your behaviours in line with what you expect from your employees?	Y	N
4.	Do you live up to your potential every day?	Y	N
5.	Do you take time for personal reflection on a regular basis?	Y	N
6.	Do you search for challenges to grow professionally and personally?	Y	N
7.	Are you using your position of authority to gain agreement fairly?	Y	N
8.	Are you consistent in your behaviours?	Y	N

Chances are, there are areas in which you need improvement. If you answered 'no' to any of the questions above, you have some work to do. Walking the talk is not easy. As long as you are aware that your actions will determine the success or failure of your team's productivity, you should be able to make a daily practice of walking the talk.

You will be wise to make sure that your actions demonstrate the desired result! Whatever you say you believe in and expect your employees to emulate, you must do first.

⚡ DISCOVER YOUR LEADERSHIP STYLE

Knowing your preferred style of leadership will have an impact on your ability to lead effectively. Discover more about your style by completing this L E A D Profile leadership assessment. There is no one style that is better than another. The key is to focus on building your strengths.

In the lists below, circle one word on each row that best describes you. When evaluating each word, be totally truthful with yourself, as there is a tendency to only choose the words you like or assume to be positive. This assessment is for you to discover more about who you are, so realistically assess each word.

L	E	A	D
Extroverted	Exacting	Influential	Competitive
Confident	Thorough	Caring	Dogmatic
Impulsive	Withdrawn	Reflective	Judgemental
Expressive	Limited	Flowing	Deliberate
Persuasive	Precise	Flexible	Focused
Open	Quiet	Decisive	Traditional
Risk taker	Reserved	Team-oriented	Stubborn
Energetic	Industrious	Perceptive	Effective
Pushy	Meticulous	Impractical	Intimidating
Personable	Moderate	Proactive	Dependable
Restless	Sullen	Hasty	Rigid
Manipulative	Inexpressive	Unreasonable	Ego-driven
Impatient	Risk avoider	Intolerant	Harsh
Animated	Calm	Open	Controlled
Insistent	Modest	Supportive	Very direct
Inspiring	Serious	Objective	Ambitious
Careless	Unyielding	Opinionated	Belligerent
Outgoing	Organised	Adaptive	Persistent
Overbearing	Stuffy	Demanding	Self-critical
Abrasive	Picky	Emotional	Autocratic
Stimulating	Moralistic	Approachable	Tough
Reactive	Expecting	Agreeable	Insensitive
Egotistic	Vigilant	Determined	Assertive
Enthusiastic	Accurate	Involving	Efficient
Audacious	Logical	Concerned	Distant
Creative	Factual	Sensitive	Independent
Impulsive	Cautious	People-oriented	Critical
Dramatic	Uninvolved	Ingratiating	Aggressive
Friendly	Specific	Compassionate	Goal-oriented
Spontaneous	Detached	Intuitive	Strong-willed
Adventurous	Detailed	Reliable	Results-driven

🎇 Interpret Your Score

Add up the total number of words in each column. The quadrant with the highest total is your preferred style of leadership. If quadrants have the same total, this indicates that you have a more blended style of leadership and tend to adapt your style to the situation.

L column: _____

E column: _____

A column: _____

D column: _____

L E A D PROFILE

LEVERAGER	EXACTER
ADAPTOR	DIRECTOR

People-oriented   *Task-oriented*

THE LEVERAGER

STRENGTHS	WEAKNESSES	LIKES
• People-oriented	• Talks too much	• Recognition
• Persuasive verbal skills	• Loud or aggressive	• Spontaneity in developing ideas
• Likes involvement	• Emotional or erratic	• Broad overview
• Quick decision maker	• Not detail-oriented	• Quick interactive meetings
• Aware of others' emotions	• Uncontrollable	• Working with others
• Highly competitive	• Disorganised	• Risk taking

THE EXACTER

STRENGTHS	WEAKNESSES	LIKES
• Problem solver	• Accumulates too much information	• Facts, statistics, figures
• Steady and deliberate	• Procrastinates	• Well-presented information
• Not distracted by emotion	• Unwilling to offer opinions	• Time to think and process
• Orderly and systematic	• Uncommunicative	• Efficiency
• Knowledgeable	• Too serious	• Working autonomously
• Thorough	• Reluctant to approach others	• Accountability

THE ADAPTOR

STRENGTHS	WEAKNESSES	LIKES
• People skills	• Disorganised	• Relationship building
• Approachable	• Easily bored	• Support of others
• Cooperative and easygoing	• Relentless	• Change
• Flexible	• High expectations of others	• To be listened to
• Highly intuitive	• Dislikes waiting	• Involvement
• Team-oriented	• Intolerant	• Collaboration

THE DIRECTOR

STRENGTHS	WEAKNESSES	LIKES
• Task-oriented	• Lacks patience	• To be in control
• Ambitious	• Inadvertently inconsiderate of others	• Clearly defined goals and objectives
• Take-charge approach	• Easily bored	• Winning
• Enjoys challenges	• Hates losing	• Achieving results
• Organised	• Resents lazy people	• Competitive situations
• Decisive	• Critical	• Projects completed correctly and on time

KNOW YOUR DESTINATION

What distinguishes a company and its individuals is the relentless pursuit of compelling ideas through vision. When you have a well-defined vision of where you want to go, the journey becomes clear.

If you don't know where you are going, how will you know when you get there? It is recognised worldwide that a leader who provides direction and support to his employees really sparks the desire in employees to perform at their optimum. Leadership expert Julie Morgan, owner of Thrive Consulting in Las Vegas, says, 'It takes hard, constant, consistent work on oneself to create and communicate a vision that, once shared, becomes a road map of success for all team members.'

Employees who have a purpose and a direction will have reasons to be creative and innovative! Jack Welch, former CEO of General Electric, fervently describes vision: 'Good leaders create a vision, articulate the vision, passionately own the vision and relentlessly drive it to completion.' Gifted leaders know how to take hold of the dream inside of them and transplant it in others.

In 1961, President John F Kennedy challenged his nation to send a man to the moon before the end of the decade. This goal was considered to be outrageous, and scientific capabilities at that time gave no reason for optimism. He had so ardently communicated the reason for this challenge that the whole country was mobilised into reaching this goal. By July of 1969, his vision became a reality.

Sharing your vision, your mental picture of the future, with people who are going to help you create results will give them something with which they can resonate. For your vision to become a reality, invite your team members to participate by getting their input and soliciting feedback. Employees who are informed and feel that they are included are more likely to cooperate, take ownership and think creatively. When you don't involve your team members, they are unlikely to participate fully and passionately in the attainment of your vision.

Vision serves as a psychological lighthouse that gives purpose to life and added meaning to what we do. It is the guide your team members need to achieve results. The happiest

'Give us a clear vision that we may know where to stand and what to stand for, because unless we stand for something, we shall fall for anything.' Peter Marshall

'I find that the great thing in the world is not only where we stand, but also in what direction we are moving.'
Oliver Wendell Holmes

employees are those who have clear objectives and the necessary support to enable them to do their jobs. In many companies, managers spend very little time coaching employees. It is the role of managers to 'coach,' 'support' and 'mentor' their employees well. People perform better if they have clearly defined responsibilities and the support they need.

One of the most important steps in the creative process is to make sure that you're focusing on the desired solution or objective. This is where many people go wrong! By not stating clear goals and objectives, you and your team members are likely to head in different and sometimes wrong directions. That would be like competing in a race but in the wrong race! The result is that your team fails in being able to create usable, valuable ideas or successful solutions.

To arrive at new and worthwhile destinations, it is crucial to define the destinations. Going in one direction, no matter how efficiently, won't get you where you want to go if it is the wrong direction. Imagine if you were heading towards a specific location and you took a wrong road by mistake. It would not matter how well, how long or how fast you drove. You would never reach your destination.

A player, Roy Riegels, playing in a classic Rose Bowl football game between California and Georgia Tech, grabbed a loose ball and took off running. He was able to elude his tacklers by cutting in and out with incredible athleticism. He was tackled by one of his own teammates one yard away from the goal line as he was sprinting the distance of the field. Roy Riegels had somehow lost his bearings and run the wrong way! From that moment on, Roy Riegels earned the reputation of 'Wrong Way' Riegels rather than being remembered for his astonishing athletic abilities!

Similarly, it is essential to clearly define a problem or

What's the use of running, if you're running on the wrong road?
German proverb

12

clearly outline your objective – to be pointed in the right direction – if you are to create a solution. You and your team must be able to move step by step towards the correct goal for a successful, creative result.

Take your team into the future by sharing your vision. Show them where you want to go, then bring them back. Then they will figure out how to get there by themselves. Let them see the big picture and get a sense of the importance of their contribution to it. Tell them what outcome you want to accomplish, let them hear you say where you want to go. They need direction! To deliver results, involve your team. Employee involvement is enlisting the knowledge, skill and excitement of your employees. Walt Disney was quoted as saying, 'You can dream, create, design and build the most wonderful place in the world, but it requires people to make the dream a reality.'

BE PATIENT

Because our team members are our most important competitive advantage, more emphasis needs to be put on helping them grow. Growth means change. When you make changes and you challenge people to get out of their 'comfort zone,' having patience will pay off! Rarely is a person able to hit a nail on its head and drive it in fully with a single blow. Usually, the way to drive a nail in straight and firm is through repeated blows. The same is true when developing your team's creative thinking and changing the culture. Don't expect perfection. With careful instruction and clear objectives, your team will become more productive and you will profit.

In a time gone by, there were two Arab boys, Yazid and Haroun, who as young friends shared many adventures in their village and the nearby desert. As they became young men, they

> 'A blind man's world is bounded by the limits of his touch; an ignorant man's world by the limits of his knowledge; a great man's world by the limits of his vision.'
> E. Paul Harvey

> 'Patience is the art of concealing your impatience.'
> Unknown

went their separate ways. Haroun became a wealthy man, whereas Yazid became a poor rope maker.

Years passed by. One day Yazid was in the streets of Baghdad selling his ropes when he came face to face with Haroun. Haroun was ecstatic and immediately offered Yazid a position in his court as the royal date merchant. Yazid was delighted and accepted the position immediately. His job was to select only the finest dates in the land for the sheik, Haroun.

Yazid went immediately to find only the finest dates and returned a week later with a load of dates he believed to be of the highest quality. The sheik's advisers sampled the fruit and were horrified to discover that they were not of the finest quality but rather quite inferior. They immediately wanted to discharge Yazid. Haroun admonished his advisers, saying to them, 'You do not understand Yazid. He has lived all of his life in poverty, and he has no way of differentiating high-quality dates from inferior dates. Yazid believed he had only the best dates. We must be patient with Yazid and teach him to know the difference between good dates and bad dates.' So Haroun instructed his advisers, 'From now on, you are to give Yazid a few dates for dinner. I want you to begin by giving him low-quality dates and gradually give him better dates. After a while he will know the difference because he will be able to taste the difference. When this is understood by Yazid, I guarantee you that he will bring us only the finest dates in the land.'

Haroun was able to prove to his advisers that the time invested in his employee would pay off. With this new knowledge, Yazid was able to raise his standards. All because his leader, Haroun, had taken the time and had the patience to develop his potential. This story illustrates what an effective leader can accomplish by helping an individual realise his potential.

Patience will be necessary when you start changing the way things have always been done. New ideas can be threatening because they bring change when they are implemented. They challenge the comfort zone of most people. The response of society in most cases is to repel new ideas and ways. The 'good old days' are preferable to moving into something new, unfamiliar, uncomfortable and scary. Be patient.

LISTEN AND LEARN FROM YOUR EMPLOYEES

When you encourage employees to become more solution-oriented and to be on the lookout for better ways of doing things, you will need to be receptive to what they tell you. You will need to listen and respond to them.

'Sticking to it is the genius!'
Thomas Edison

Effective communication requires understanding and the ability to be a good listener. Listening is considered to be the single most important communication skill. It will help you to understand the other person's point of view as well as show your team members that you care! Making a practice of genuinely listening is the key to effective communication and trust. It is one of the most vital attributes of an effective leader.

Many years ago, Loyola University of Chicago conducted a survey of thousands of workers asking, 'What makes an effective manager?' The number one answer was, 'One who listens to the individual employee'. The number two answer was, 'Creates an environment in which we can talk freely with our boss!' An employee will most likely talk to someone who listens and is patient. All too often we listen only with the intent to reply. We are so busy formulating our reply that the message we are supposed to receive is often missed. Instead, if we were to make a practice of listening with intent and listening before speaking, we would have better understanding!

'A good
listener is
not only
popular
everywhere,
but after a
while he
knows
something.'
Wilson
Mizner

Thomas Edison, at a time in his life when he was at a dead end, once asked his janitor this question, 'What do you think I should do about this situation?' The janitor was quite plainly stunned and replied, 'Nobody ever asked me for my advice before.' Edison's response was, 'Then you should have a lot of good ideas stored up.'

Stop, look, listen and assess what's going on. Listen to what is being voiced. You'll learn how your team members feel and find out what their desires and needs are. Listening openly one-on-one or by paying attention to conversations going on around you will give you incredible information. Be sure to include customers and 'stakeholders' on your list of people to whom you listen. Never underestimate the power of listening.

Frieda Caplan, founder of Frieda's Finest, which is a successful and flourishing produce company in a highly competitive marketplace where generic products reign, has established brand identity and uniqueness. She has achieved this because she listened to her customers' wants and needs and supplied them with unusual fruits and vegetables. A customer once asked her if she had ever heard of the Chinese gooseberry. She replied that she had not and promised to keep a lookout. Coincidentally, a supplier offered her a load of Chinese gooseberries shortly thereafter. She observed that these fruits were not particularly visually appealing. To sell them successfully, she would need some good marketing and public relations. The fruit was renamed kiwi fruit, which today is a well-known and sought-after fruit. Listening to her customers brought her endless opportunities that might well have been missed otherwise.

Poor listening is abundant! Have you ever considered how well you listen? Dr Ralph Nichols, an authority on listening, found through extensive research and studies that most people listen at about a 30 per cent rate of efficiency. It is a skill that can be easily learned.

If you want to be understood and listened to as a leader, you have to listen to your team members first. Listening will help you develop your ability to understand and respond proactively. When you don't listen, you may lose out on many meaningful opportunities, or even squander an opportunity to learn from the experience of others.

When it comes to dealing with people, effective communication with emphasis on the skill of listening is critical to a successful outcome. John D Rockefeller once made this comment: 'The ability to deal with people is as perishable as sugar and coffee, and I will pay more for that ability than for any other under the sun.'

 **SELF-ASSESSMENT**

This assessment is intended to help you think about the need of vision and how vital it is to smart business practices. Vision transforms life.

1. How do you define vision?

_____

_____

2. Who is the most visionary leader you've ever known? What specifically was it about this person that you admired?

_____

_____

3. State your current vision. _____

_____

4. Do you involve and discuss your vision frequently with those who are under your leadership?

_____

_____

5. What are your obstacles? _____

_____

_____

6. Describe why you feel the vision you are pursuing is so important.

_____

_____

7. When you have achieved your vision, what will have changed for you and your team members?

_____

_____

RECOGNISE AND REWARD CREATIVITY

Recognition can be the spark that fires peak personal performance, outstanding accomplishment and creativity. In order to nurture creativity, you must consistently recognise employee skills and behaviours. Your role as a leader is to consistently recognise your employees for the good work they do. As Ken Blanchard says in the *One Minute Manager*, 'Make a habit of catching people doing something right'. Not only will it make them feel good, but it will also change the spirit in your place of work when you begin to truly appreciate your team members' abilities. To maximise creativity within your organisation, you must encourage your employees to think conceptually. Be sure to reward them when they have accomplished this. What gets celebrated gets repeated. Outstanding leaders recognise and reward achievement!

Jack Welch, former CEO of General Electric, says, 'Any company trying to compete must find ways to engage the mind of every employee.' People want to work for organisations that value them and enhance their lives. There are many studies which show that the key reason why people work is to feel appreciated. Yet, study after study has shown that the major deprivation in the workplace is recognition. 'People will be loyal when they feel appreciated,' according to motivational guru Zig Ziglar. Think about how you feel when your achievement has been recognised. You feel as though you can do just about anything. Conversely, when your achievement has been ignored, you lose your desire. So it is with your employees!

Recognising and rewarding successes will help your team members use their thinking capabilities. Create a work environment where recognition is practised on a daily basis. Good ideas need to be noticed. Successful leaders make a habit of letting team members know that their ideas and input are valued.

Try any of these 12 EASY ways to recognise and reward people:

1. **Make an appointment to give recognition.** This gives employees something to look forward to and increases the impact of recognition.
2. **Be a 'credit giver'.** Whenever possible, make a big deal of giving credit to the people who deserve it. This will get a lot more trust and commitment than you can imagine!
3. **Carry a big carrot.** The carrot always wins over the stick. Eliminate carrying a big stick and give them incentives instead. This will encourage team members to involve themselves and initiate change.
4. **Build on past successes.** Focus on what's been done well rather than on what hasn't been done, in order to help your employees 'do it well again'.
5. **Heart and soul.** Care enough about your employees to let them know their jobs are important to the whole company.
6. **MMFI – 'make me feel important'.** When you make your employees feel important, they feel valued. This is conducive to improving performance in the workplace.
7. **Give a personal note of thanks.** This is one of your most powerful, effective and long-lasting forms of recognition. When it is in writing, it is tangible. Recipients can look at it again and again. They can show it to others. They can frame it and hang it on the wall. This supports the 'make me feel important' factor.
8. **Celebrate with a good-idea award for every idea that saves money or makes money.** Reward each suggestion that is implemented, no matter how small.
9. **MIP – 'make it public'.** Maximise input by making recognition public. This will raise pride in the person receiving

recognition and will give others the desire to receive recognition as well.

10. **Build on strengths.** By focusing on what employees do well, you are effectively a confidence builder, and confidence is the key to performance.

11. **Positive framing is giving feedback in a positive manner.** If something goes wrong, put a positive spin on it and use it as a learning experience. Find something positive in order to encourage the person to take another risk.

12. **Honour day.** One day a month is allocated to employee appreciation for any employees who have made outstanding contributions.

Frequent praise is a vital ingredient for creating an environment where employees are happy and more productive. Motivation is vital to creativity. Recognise your employees daily instead of just once a year when it is performance-review time. People need to hear praise often.

Celebrate every achievement because positive reinforcement generates positive behaviours. You will know you have done this right when ideas are flowing freely and being implemented!

You cannot afford to waste the brainpower of your team members. They need to be recognised, encouraged and supported for their efforts. Many people think of themselves as stupid. Others are afraid of incurring negative feedback. Both of these types of people will not act on their ideas and will stifle their own creativity. It is up to you to positively recognise their contributions. This will make them feel valued, and they will contribute more. A behaviour rewarded is a behaviour repeated.

Rewarding and recognising accomplishment will help you create a culture of people more willing to go out of their way to

> 'To say "well done" to any bit of good work is to take hold of the powers which have made the effort and strengthen them beyond our knowledge.'
> Phillip Brooks

do better! Recognition is critical to self-esteem. You will be amazed at what people are able to accomplish if they believe in themselves.

KNOW YOURSELF

One of your biggest competitive advantages is knowing yourself. The more you are able to understand yourself, the better equipped you are to deal with issues and problems on a daily basis, especially those that take you out of your comfort zone. Self-knowledge allows you to change any of your own inhibiting actions and unleash your creative abilities.

An effective leader makes the practice of self-evaluation a habit. It is quite surprising that only a small percentage of people in leadership positions actually do this. Leaders would greatly improve their effectiveness with their team members if they made a habit of doing this regularly. When you know more about who and what you are, situations are not so threatening. The tendency to disguise your fears is reduced.

The more you study and observe yourself, the more likely you are to increase your understanding of why you do things the way you do. Sometimes the way we do things can be to our detriment.

A CEO had a limited knowledge of technology and perpetually bragged about not needing to have or to use technology. He did this especially when he was in meetings with his employees. When the conversation became more directed towards technology, the more apparent his behaviour became. He was very obviously out of his depth. This ultimately affected the flow of communication negatively. The CEO's insecurity was merely 'disguised' by his braggart behaviour. On the face of it, his behaviour may not have appeared to be harmful.

> 'Being entirely honest with oneself is a good exercise.'
> Sigmund Freud

However, the consequences of his actions were extremely detrimental to effectively leading a team. He unwittingly conveyed the following message to his staff: 'Since I don't need to know this stuff, it's OK not to develop yourself!'

It is important for you as a leader to gain inner knowledge about yourself. The more you know about yourself, the more effectively you can lead others.

When you are willing to expand your comfort zone and adopt new approaches to your thinking, you will effect changes in your actions. Take in NEW information as often as possible. You can do this by reading, observing, listening and participating in any activity that introduces you to new ways of doing things. This will ultimately have an impact on your self-esteem and self-confidence, and you will be able to free yourself from unnecessary fears, insecurities and behaviours. Eliminating self-defeating behaviours will become your conduit for effective and positive change.

A changing world calls for a new paradigm and new methods. You'll find that old approaches, which have previously worked for you, may now be ineffective. The leaders who survive will be the ones who adapt and quickly reinvent their thinking. Leadership development is an ongoing process. It involves practice, feedback and self-awareness.

At one time, comedian Bob Hope was one of the most famous and recognisable names in the world. Throughout his career he kept reinventing himself, which was considered to have been the secret to his success. He started out in the entertainment business as a travelling vaudeville performer. From there, he moved to Broadway where he starred in many musical comedies. He then became a movie star, a radio personality and eventually succeeded in television. With each transition, Bob Hope adapted his approach from singing and dancing to

'The illiterate of the 21st century will not be those who cannot read and write, but those who cannot learn, unlearn and relearn.'
Alvin Toffler

'If you want to truly understand something, try to change it.'
Kurt Lewin

23

verbal comedy and to sight gags. He learned to deliver whatever the medium called for, unlike so many other entertainers who fell by the wayside.

To know and understand yourself includes developing a foundation of skill sets and actions that result in a more potent and effective leadership style. Consider making an appointment with yourself every month to spend 30 minutes evaluating ways in which you can reinvent yourself.

When evaluating yourself, you will eventually become more and more aware of your natural strengths. The more you know about yourself, the more you will be able to develop yourself. You will need the same dedication as if you were a coach developing your players. Spend time improving your strengths and reducing your weaknesses so that you can win the game. There is an old Chinese saying: 'Develop your strengths to the fullest and your weaknesses become unimportant'. Make a practice of focusing on your strengths and you will find that your weaknesses will diminish. Skills will become second nature to you as they are practised.

You should continuously find ways to enhance your own talents, skills and knowledge. It's not an option. Make a commitment to yourself to start investing at least 1 per cent of your time in learning to understand more thoroughly the way you think and feel. You will find that this small investment in time will pay huge dividends in your effectiveness as both a leader and an individual.

'The life which is not examined is not worth living.'
Plato

SELF-EVALUATION

1. How do you think others perceive you?

   _____

   _____

2. How well do you know yourself?

   _____

   _____

3. What triggers your fears?

   _____

   _____

4. On a scale of 1 to 10, how would you rate yourself as a leader or manager?

   _____

   _____

5. How would you be functioning differently if you had rated yourself a 10? (Answer this question only if you didn't score yourself a 10)

   _____

   _____

6. What things are you doing to grow?

   _____

   _____

7. Are you open to ideas from others?

   _____

   _____

8. How do you respond to resistance from others?

   _____

   _____

9. What makes you overreact to situations?

   _____

   _____

10. What three things would you change about the way you lead others to make you a more effective leader or manager?

   _____

   _____

11. For the next five days, observe what happens to you when things go wrong. How do you react?

   _____

   _____

12. If your reaction is negative, what can you change to improve your behaviour?

   _____

   _____

CHAPTER TWO

COMMUNICATE FOR RESULTS

As a leader, you know whether you have communicated effectively by what is understood and what ultimately gets done! Therefore, every aspect of your communication should be in alignment with your purpose to create a culture of team members who think creatively.

Communication is the number one problem in organisations. For that matter, it's also the number one problem in our personal lives. Without a doubt, good communication is the most crucial element to sustaining creativity and motivation in the workplace. Open lines of communication will create more levels of understanding and trust. As the levels of trust increase, there will be a dramatic increase in creativity and innovation.

When you do not communicate effectively, there will be limited understanding. A precise communication strategy needs to be developed to ensure that your team members have a win-win approach to communication.

Southwest Airlines' management believes that a lack of communication creates confusion and misunderstanding. Therefore, the airline's employees have immediate access to critical information so that they are better able to serve customers and reduce problems. Take a look at Southwest Airlines' customer service compared with other airlines. Southwest Airlines' employees are known for providing extraordinary service, having fun while they work, adhering

> 'How well we communicate is not determined by how well we say things but by how well we speak and are understood.'
> Andrew Grove

to a strong work ethic, and being dedicated to their jobs and their company.

GETTING TO KNOW YOUR PEOPLE

Good communication occurs when there is mutual understanding. It also means having an understanding of what makes your employees think, feel and act the way they do. It is one of the most powerful tools you can have for motivating your team members to make decisive changes. It is amazing how difficult it can sometimes be to get a point across. Equally amazing is how differently people hear the same message.

Understanding your team members and their personalities is vital to the communication process. Know what motivates your employees so that you can understand what drives them. (Do you know how many children they have and what their favourite pastimes are, for example?) This is very important.

If we spent more time finding out about the often overlooked little things, the payoff would be huge. Cavett Robert, founder of the National Speakers Association, is well-known for this statement: 'Your people don't care how much you know until they know how much you care.' Making the time investment to get to know and understand your team members (individually and in groups) shows that you care. It also earns the respect of your employees. You don't earn respect just because you happen to have a leadership position. Showing care and concern about team members' well-being is a small price to pay for the return on investment.

Understanding your employees' individual styles of communication will help you work better with them and assist them in being more effective in their jobs. Regularly spend one-on-one time with each member of your team. Ask such

> Say what you mean and mean what you say.

28

questions as, 'What can we do around here to help you be even more effective?' 'How are things going?' 'What ideas do you have to improve things?' Acknowledge something about them or their work that you have noticed.

Consider using specific folders or logs to record your dialogue and the feedback you receive from others. This will help you to remember important information that you may need to act upon.

You can't go wrong when you are communicating effectively. Ensure understanding by consistently involving your team members, giving feedback, asking questions and listening. The process is ongoing.

> 'The most important thing in communication is to hear what isn't being said.'
> Peter Drucker

PERCEPTION ASSESSMENT

To be effective as a leader, it is essential to assume many roles. To see how you have mastered these roles, answer the following questions by using the 1–5 scale below.

5 – Always agree
4 – Often agree
3 – Sometimes agree
2 – Rarely agree
1 – Disagree

1. I am a leader who is familiar with both the issues and challenges that my team members have in their jobs as well as their personal lives. _____

2. I know what motivates my team. _____

3. I know what skills team members have. _____

4. I set goals that are realistic for my team. _____

5. I ask for input from my team members on the goals I have set. _____

6. I regularly communicate my strategy with the members of my team so they know where they are heading. _____

7. I am good at delegating projects to my team. _____

8. I make sure that I use the strengths and attributes of my team members to complement one another. _____

9. I keep up-to-date with emerging technology to help my team members stay productive. _____

10. I am careful not to micromanage my people. _____

11. I take action on the promises I make to create trust with my team members. _____

12. I coach my people every day to encourage and support them to be the best they can be. _____

13. I praise my team members when they have done a good job. _____

14. I am careful to give constructive feedback in private. _____

15. I communicate in an effective and open manner on a consistent basis. _____

16. I manage my team to become solution-oriented when there is a problem and give direction when it is needed. _____

17. I regularly schedule one-on-one meetings with my team members. _____

18. I am an effective listener. _____

19. I am decisive and controlled when there is a problem. _____

20. My team members will support me and perform at their best when we are experiencing difficulties or deadlines that need to be met. _____

Total _____

Interpret Your Score

If your score is below 39, it will be wise to further develop your skills in management and leadership.

If you have a score between 40 and 64, you're on your way to being an effective leader and need to focus on developing your skills in your weakest areas.

If you have a score between 65 and 90, you are an effective leader and can still improve your skills for better results.

If your score is between 91 and 100, you are exceptional! It will be wise not to become complacent. Keep developing yourself as an overall strategy to maintain your leadership advantage.

AWARENESS AND UNDERSTANDING

Jan Carlzon, CEO of Scandinavian Airlines, says, 'You have to calculate in your intuitions about people – your sense of their reactions, their feelings.' What better way to do this than to recognise and understand their behaviours.

The more you know about what makes up the personalities of your team members, the more likely you are to tap into their creativity and show them how they can use their own thinking abilities to work more effectively. There are many instruments available in the marketplace for assessing personality styles: Myers-Briggs, DISC, I-Opt. We use the SELF Profile, which will help you to better understand yourself and others on and off the job.

Each of us is unique. We all have different perceptions, values and experiences. The SELF Profile is a survey of social style that is designed to:

- Identify the particular style that you most often use in personal interactions.
- Help you gain a better understanding of yourself and others.
- Help you predict how you and others respond in given situations.
- Improve your communication with others who have different styles and build more meaningful relationships.

The SELF Profile has four distinct social styles of interaction with others. All of us are a blend of ALL four styles, but you will be able to identify your own dominant style and the dominant style of each of your team members. SELF was developed using the most sophisticated techniques available, but it cannot provide accurate feedback if you do not provide accurate responses. Therefore, it is best to answer the questions in the way that you behave now, rather than the way you used to be or would most like to be. Remember, no personality style is better than any other. Honest answers will provide you with the most accurate, useful information possible.

SELF DIRECTIONS

The SELF Profile consists of 30 general questions describing how a person might act in a given situation.
- For questions 1–24, use the 1–5 scale listed below to describe how you might act in a given situation.
- For questions 25–30, choose A or B – whichever response describes you the best.

Please place the number that best describes you on the line at the end of each question.

	Not at all like me	Somewhat like me	Occasionally like me	Usually like me	Very much like me
	1	2	3	4	5

1. When in a group, I tend to speak and act as the representative of that group. _____

2. I am seldom quiet when I am with other people. _____

3. When faced with a leadership position, I tend to actively accept that role rather than diffusing it among others. _____

4. I would rather meet new people than read a good book. _____

5. Sometimes I ask more from my friends or family than they can accomplish. _____

6. I enjoy going out frequently. _____

7. It's important to me that people follow the advice I give them. _____

8. I like to entertain guests. _____

9. When I am in charge of a situation, I am comfortable assigning others to specific tasks. _____

10. I often go out of my way to meet new people. _____

11. In social settings, I find myself asking more questions of others than they ask of me. _____

12. I truly enjoy mixing in a crowd. _____

13. Other people usually think of me as being energetic. _____

14. I make friends very easily. _____

15. I am a verbal person. _____

16. I try to be supportive of my friends, no matter what they do. _____

17. When I see that things aren't going smoothly in a group, I usually take the lead and try to bring some structure to the situation. _____

18. I seldom find it hard to really enjoy myself at a lively party. _____

19. When in a leadership position, I like to clearly define my role and let followers know what is expected. _____

20. I consider myself to be good at small talk. _____

21. I am very good at persuading others to see things my way. _____

22. I can usually let myself go and have fun with friends. _____

23. I often find myself playing the role of leader and taking charge of the situation. _____

24. I do not prefer the simple, quiet life. _____

For questions 25–30, please write the letter representing your response on the line at the beginning of each question.

_____ 25. I am in a conversation with more than one person. Someone makes a statement that I know is incorrect, but I am sure the others didn't catch it. Do I let the others know?
A. Yes
B. No

_____ 26. After a hard day's work I prefer to:
A. Get together with friends and do something active.
B. Relax at home and read or watch TV.

_____ 27. When planning a social outing with a small group, I am most likely to:
A. Be the first to suggest some plans and try to get others to quickly make a decision.
B. Make sure everyone has a say in the planning and go along with what the group decides.

_____ 28. I have finished a three-month project for which I have sacrificed a great deal of my free time and energy. To celebrate, I am more likely to:

> A. Invite some of my friends over and throw a party.
>
> B. Spend a quiet, peaceful weekend doing whatever I wish, either by myself or with a special friend.

_____ 29. If I feel that I am underpaid for my work, I'm most likely to:

> A. Confront the boss and demand a raise.
>
> B. Do nothing and hope the situation improves.

_____ 30. I think that those around me see me primarily as:

> A. Gregarious and outgoing.
>
> B. Introspective and thoughtful.

Score Your SELF Profile

1. On items 25–30:
   - If you answered A, give yourself a 5.
   - If you answered B, give yourself a 1.
2. Now transfer each of the scores to the blanks below.
3. Add each column

1. _____	2. _____
3. _____	4. _____
5. _____	6. _____
7. _____	8. _____
9. _____	10. _____
11. _____	12. _____
13. _____	14. _____
15. _____	16. _____
17. _____	18. _____
19. _____	20. _____
21. _____	22. _____
23. _____	24. _____
25. _____	26. _____
27. _____	28. _____
29. _____	30. _____
Total _____	Total _____
_____ Directive score	_____ Affiliative score

3. Add each column.

If you scored from:	Give yourself:
15–21	1
22–33	2
34–44	3
45–56	4
57–68	5
69–75	6

- Take your Directive Score and put a dot on the broken line below.
- Then put a dot on the dotted line below for your Affiliative Score.
- Next, connect the dots with a straight line.
- Shade in the area between the line you've drawn and the intersection of the broken and dotted lines.

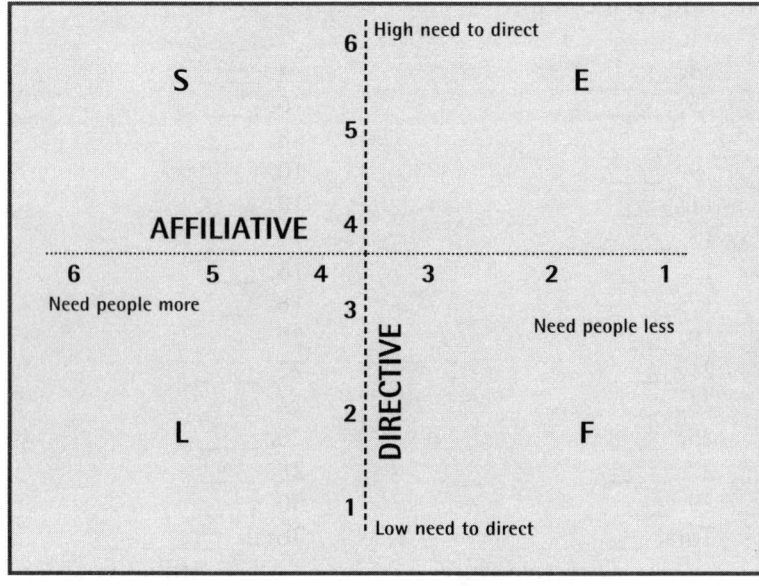

SELF Characteristics

Below are some of the characteristics that can be used to describe the tendencies of each dimension of the SELF.

STRENGTHS

	HIGH		
S	Persuasive	E	Practical
	Risk taker		Orderly
	Competitive		Very direct
	Pursues change		Self-determined
	Confident		Organised
	Socially skilled		Traditional
	Inspiring		Goal-oriented
	Open		Dependable
	Direct		Economical
	Outgoing		Ambitious

HIGH — AFFILIATIVE — LOW / DIRECTIVE

L	Team-oriented	F	Exacting
	Caring		Thorough
	Devoted		Factual
	Enthusiastic		Reserved
	Helpful		Meticulous
	Accessible		Practical
	Trusting		Calm
	Sensitive		Has high standards
	Good listener and friend		Risk-avoider
	Likes variety		
	Gregarious		
	Peacemaker		

LOW

LIMITATIONS

	HIGH		
S	Pushy	E	Dogmatic
	Intimidating		Stubborn
	Overbearing		Rigid
	Restless		Unapproachable
	Impatient		Distant
	Manipulative		Critical
	Abrasive		Insensitive
	Reactive		
	Dominating		

HIGH — AFFILIATIVE — LOW / DIRECTIVE

L	Too other-oriented	F	Slow to get things done
	Indecisive		Perfectionistic
	Impractical		Withdrawn
	Vulnerable		Dull
	Hesitant		Sullen
	Subjective		Shy
			Passive

LOW

SELF and Interactions With Others

TURN-ONS

	HIGH		
S	Attention	E	Control
	Achievement		Responsibility
	Recognition		Mastery
	Adventure		Loyalty
	Excitement		Fast pace
	Spontaneity		

HIGH — AFFILIATIVE — LOW / DIRECTIVE

L	Popularity	F	Perfection
	Closeness		Autonomy
	Affirmation		Consistency
	Kindness		Practical things
	Caring		Information

LOW

TURN-OFFS

	HIGH		
S	Waiting	E	Ambiguity
	Indecision		Irreverence
	Convention		Laziness
	Lack of enthusiasm		Showing emotions

HIGH — AFFILIATIVE — LOW / DIRECTIVE

L	Insensitivity	F	Aggressiveness
	Dissension		Carelessness
	Insincerity		Arrogance
	Egotism		Fakes

LOW

Now that you have completed the SELF Profile, you have access to more information for understanding others. Following are guidelines to assist you in using this information.

- The information in this assessment is designed to aid you in self-awareness and in understanding others in broad and general terms.
- Always remember that an individual's behaviour is greatly affected by the situation she is in. You can expect individuals to exhibit a variety of different characteristics in different situations.
- It will help you to remember that an individual's social style is the product of many years' development and is not easily changed.
- With your understanding of the differences in the way people communicate, you will be able to use this information to get the best from your team.

> If you want something different, then do something different!

COMMUNICATE VISUALLY

Graphics and other visuals illuminate your written communications. Change documentation, such as memos, letters and reports, to include graphics, cartoons, quotations and pictures. The visual aspect conveys your message with more impact and is an effective and memorable way to share your information. It is important that the visual is appropriate to the documentation. If you are giving an employee a disciplinary document, using a cartoon is not a good idea!

Visual aids, in various forms, can be used to boost creativity. As you add a new creative spirit to these communications, performance will improve significantly.

Frank Kohn of Kohn Graphics has created an organisation wherein open and honest communication is the cardinal rule of a healthy workplace. In order to involve all of his employees, he places a chart in a common area accessible to all employees for them to see revenue targets. When the goal is achieved, a symbol depicting the value of revenue is placed on the graphic for everyone to see. By communicating goals in this manner, Frank Kohn has created more competitive interest and motivation for his people to progress in a fun and creative way.

Visual communications can also be used to find solutions. Consider giving everyone a box of crayons and a sheet of paper. Ask them to illustrate any problems they may have by drawing a picture that can be discussed in a meeting.

Infinity Transportation was having performance issues with some of its employees. Al Hunt, a manager, found a way to solve the problem. He came up with the idea of showing his people the performance standards by which he was measured: the goals and objectives.

By using whiteboards and green and red markers, he was visually able to show his employees their impact on the job. He used the green markers to depict positive measures and red markers for negative measures. In the beginning, the visual measurement was displayed primarily in red. However, the employees knew the goal was to get in the green. Departments began to compete with one another, and before long, standards were displayed primarily in green! The goal of improved performance was achieved.

CHAPTER THREE

UNDERSTANDING DIFFERENT THINKING STYLES

In today's business climate, the leader with only one way to do things is usually stuck in a rut. Getting your team to apply different thinking approaches to generate new ideas and solutions to problems is essential to the survival and growth of your organisation.

Developing your team members' thinking skills is one of the most important investments you can make. Many of your team members have an untapped potential that just needs to be exercised. Thinking is a skill that can be learned, practised, developed and improved.

A BRIEF HISTORY

Aristotle, a distinguished Greek philosopher (384–322 BC), understood the brain to be an organ to cool the blood! Socrates, one of the greatest thinkers of all time (469–399 BC), believed true knowledge was derived from dialogue and systematic questioning.

Sigmund Freud (1856–1939) ascertained that there was a lot more to the brain and its power than was originally thought. He proposed that two patterns of thinking existed, which he termed 'primary process' thinking and 'secondary process' thinking.

Over time, others challenged Freud, claiming that there are

additional patterns of thought. One of them was Carl Jung, a Swiss psychiatrist and psychologist (1875–1961), who based his theory of thinking on four psychological functions:

1. Sensing
2. Intuition
3. Thinking
4. Feeling

DEFINING INTELLIGENCE

Research by French psychologist Alfred Binet (1857–1911) established the first scientific and authentic method for measuring intelligence. IQ tests, as they are called, were accepted without question until the 1970s when research by Professor Howard Gardner and Professor Robert Ornstein determined that there are multiple intelligences that play a role in a human being's IQ, or intelligence quotient.

These multiple intelligences include the following:

- **Verbal/linguistic intelligence** – the processing of information through written and spoken words.
- **Visual/spatial intelligence** – the ability to form mental pictures and images.
- **Logical/mathematical intelligence** – the capacity to recognise patterns, find connections, separate pieces of information and work with abstract symbols, numbers and shapes.
- **Bodily/kinesthetic intelligence** – the ability to use the body to express emotion and ideas as well as practise hands-on activities.
- **Musical/rhythmic intelligence** – the capacity to recognise and use rhythmic and tonal patterns.
- **Interpersonal intelligence** – the ability to communicate well with people.

- **Intrapersonal intelligence** – the ability to understand one's own thinking processes and feelings, to view oneself objectively.
- **Naturalistic intelligence** – the ability to identify with the environment and understand one's relationship to animals, plants and all of nature.

Howard Gardner and Robert Ornstein also determined that real intelligence means using all of the brain to engage all of these types of intelligence to live life completely and fully.

THEORIES OF THINKING

In the 1950s, JP Guilford introduced the theories of 'divergent thinking' and 'convergent thinking'. Divergent thinking is an individual's ability to use imagination to generate multiple ideas and expand alternatives to solve a problem. Convergent thinking focuses on a solution to a problem and the ability to use logic and judgement to evaluate and narrow down alternatives. Using both divergent and convergent thinking is essential to solving problems and making decisions effectively.

A simple analogy that gives a good perspective and understanding of using these thinking skills is appropriately defined by Karl Albrecht, author of *The Creative Corporation*: 'Divergent thinking is like using a wide-angle lens; with it you see the whole view. Convergent thinking is like focusing on one detail with a telephoto lens. The ideal lens is a zoom lens, which allows one to shift back and forth between divergent and convergent thinking. The most effective and creative thinkers have this zoom-lens capability as a matter of habit. They can think divergently when necessary, and convergently when necessary.' He adds, 'Creative thinkers have their lens set for the wide angle most of the time.'

Convergent thinking is like a spotlight that is bright, clear and intense with a narrow focus. Divergent thinking is like a floodlight covering a wider area with a less intense light.

Divergent thinking is exciting because it creates possibilities for seeing things differently and generating new ideas. It is central to problem finding. It involves finding numerous connections to the situation and generating a variety of approaches. An example of divergent thinking is an architect who draws and devises various sketches for a planned building development. When the architect reaches the point where he begins to eliminate certain approaches, his thinking converges.

> 'The present serious human predicament requires all our creative energies for its resolution.'
> Dr Jonas Salk

LEFT-BRAIN AND RIGHT-BRAIN THINKING

In the early 1960s, Nobel Laureate Roger Sperry of the California Institute of Technology identified the brain's dual nature – two separate brain halves with different mental activities. The left hemisphere of the brain thinks in terms of words, symbols, numbers and lists, and processes pieces of information sequentially (the verbal and analytical mode). The right hemisphere of the brain thinks in terms of images, pictures and colours, and processes information all at once, holistically and intuitively (the visual and perceptual mode). An example is the function of memory. Remembering the name of a person is a left-brain function. Remembering a person's face is a right-brain function.

More specifically, Sperry described the characteristics of the left and right sides of the brain using the terms in the box on page 44.

Sperry also discovered that when the left side of the brain is active, the right side goes into a relaxed and semi-meditative, alpha-wave state. When the right side of the brain is active, the

Left Brain	Right Brain
(Intellectual)	*(Emotional)*
Logical	Intuitive
Verbal	Artistic
Linear	Nonlinear
Analytical	Holistic
Sequential	Visual
Convergent	Divergent
Digital	Analogical
Intellectual	Imaginative
Objective	Subjective
Rational	Emotional
Goal-oriented	Symbolic
Explicit	Spatial
Mathematical	Insightful
Deductive	Creative
Structured	Expressive
Detailed	Feeling
Practical	Multiprocessing

left side of the brain assumes the same relaxed, semi-meditative, alpha-wave state.

In the 1980s, Professor Zaidel of the University of California carried out further research based on the work of Sperry, which led to the discovery that each side of the brain has abilities of the other side. The two hemispheres are connected through a structure called the corpus callosum (bridge of nerve tissue connecting the left and right hemispheres). It is responsible for the essential communication between the two hemispheres.

Both hemispheres have complex processing abilities using many parts of the brain. The limbic system is a group of structures in the brain associated with emotions, and the cerebral cortex is the seat of higher brain functions.

USING WHOLE-BRAIN THINKING

In his book *Use Both Sides of Your Brain*, author Tony Buzan states that Albert Einstein, one of the greatest geniuses of all time, had seemed to be predominantly left-brain dominant. A more thorough investigation unearthed that Einstein was 'whole-brained', or capable of using both sides of the brain. Einstein made a regular habit of playing imagination games. He loved 'thought experiments'. He considered imagination to be infinite and a key component in thinking creatively. According to author John D MacArthur, Einstein's brain was particularly well-developed in an area known as the inferior parietal lobe, which can be found at the upper, rear part of the brain's neocortex. This area is the most evolved site in the human brain and is commonly known as 'Area 39', our higher intellect.

Leonardo da Vinci, the Italian artist, architect and engineer (1452–1519), said he became a 'genius' because he learned how his brain worked, and then he worked at using his brain! He was a self-educated man who developed all of his types of intelligence for his own betterment.

Even though some experts today argue against labelling people as being specifically left-brain or right-brain thinkers, most human beings have a dominant hemisphere. A better understanding of this, according to Tony Buzan: 'We describe ourselves as talented in certain areas and not talented in others. What we are really describing are those areas of our potential that we have successfully developed and those areas of our potential that still lie dormant, which really could, with nurturing, flourish.'

Through misinformation and miseducation, many people believe that the development of their weaker area is unobtainable. Scientists say that less than 5 per cent of people have the natural, automatic tendency to be disciplined enough to use both sides of their brains interactively, though all people have the ability. Fortunately, as a result of Sperry's research, the 'weaker' mental abilities can be improved and developed by employing techniques that require the use of both sides of the brain at once. A balance between both sides of the brain is ideal. The key is to train both sides of the brain, most especially the areas that may be weak.

ACCESSING BOTH SIDES OF THE BRAIN

'The average person thinks two or three times a year; I've made an international reputation for myself by thinking once or twice a week.'
George Bernard Shaw

Both left and right-brain thinking play an important role in the process of solving problems creatively. If you want your employees to do extraordinary things, they must be able to shift consciously from one mode of thinking to the other. This does not mean that an individual changes dominance or preference but rather develops skills to be able to use the less preferred side of the brain when needed. This is essential to increase productivity and performance. The left-brain approach will be required when you need your team to think in a more practical manner – getting things done. The right-brain approach is required when your team needs to engage in imaginative thinking – thinking differently.

There are times when the task at hand may require more of one type of thinking than the other. Successful people have learned how to use both sides of the brain, switching from 'intellectual' to 'emotional' or from 'emotional' to 'intellectual,' as required. For example: Problem solving initially requires right-brain thinking, then requires left-brain thinking for analysis and for putting a plan into action. Problem solving using only left-brain thinking won't be effective if there are not enough ideas to work with. Too many ideas (right-brain thinking), without the use of any logic, can't be evaluated and implemented. Many of us don't maximise the use of both types of thinking as effectively as we could.

'So, one's preferred creativity style is like one's eye colour: It can't be changed,' states author Charles Prather, 'but we can learn to use both sides by developing the weaker of the two and using a "whole-brained" approach.' Charles Prather embellishes the findings of Sperry by defining two other thinking styles: 'innovative thinking' and 'adaptive thinking'.

INNOVATIVE THINKING

Innovative thinking is introducing something entirely new that had not existed before. People with this style tend to challenge and to change the system they're in. As change agents, they focus on installing a new system rather than fixing an old one. They prefer doing research, creating new products, and preserving the business for the future. They don't like to work in a linear manner but rather seek novelty. Therefore, they are proficient in inventing. The Wright brothers were innovators. They were the first to accomplish their invention, the airplane.

ADAPTIVE THINKING

This kind of thinking brings a high immediate value to any business because results are seen quickly. People with this style prefer to use creativity to perfect the system they're in. They will make any system better, faster, cheaper and more efficient by modifying or altering what already exists. Therefore, they are proficient in building on the ideas that come from others or other inventions. For example, they will take the Wright brothers' invention of the airplane and create a jet plane.

'One single idea may have greater weight than the labour of all men, animals and engines for a century.'
Ralph Waldo Emerson

Your team members will fall into one of these thinking styles. Which of these two are you? Ask your team members which one of these they think they are.

As a leader, it is vital to remember that different people think differently, just as they communicate differently. With this understanding, you will be better able to utilise your team members' unique and individual talents and abilities. Often the preferred mode of thinking of your team members doesn't match the demands of their jobs. When the preferences of employees have been determined, you will be in a far better position to utilise their talents and abilities skilfully. The frustrations that prevail in managing people can be easily resolved by changing an employee's tasks and/or position to fit his preferred mode of thinking. If you want to stimulate a culture of creativity, connect the right people with the right job.

> 'Do the things you love doing and can do well.'
> Paul Torrance

🗲 THINKING-STYLE ASSESSMENT

Circle the words listed under left-brain characteristics and right-brain characteristics that best describe you. Total the number of words circled under each column. This is a subjective exercise, but you should have a general preference for the words in the left or right columns. The highest total will indicate your preferred thinking style. This assessment in no way proves that you are definitely a right-brain or left-brain thinker. It is merely a quick indicator. A more detailed and specific assessment may elaborate the findings further.

LEFT-BRAIN CHARACTERISTICS	RIGHT-BRAIN CHARACTERISTICS
Logical	Intuitive
Verbal	Artistic
Linear	Nonlinear
Analytical	Holistic
Sequential	Visual
Convergent	Divergent
Digital	Analogical
Intellectual	Imaginative
Objective	Subjective
Rational	Emotional
Goal-oriented	Symbolic
Explicit	Spatial
Mathematical	Insightful
Deductive	Creative
Structured	Expressive
Detailed	Feeling
Practical	Multiprocessing
Total _____	Total _____

LEFT-HANDED THINKING VERSUS RIGHT-HANDED THINKING

Another perspective on thinking, as expressed by author Jerome Bruner in his book *On Knowing: Essays for the Left Hand,* is that the right hand is associated with logic, reason, order, practicality and analysis, and the left hand is associated with intuition, feelings, imagination and sensitivity. Because the left side of the brain controls the right hand and the right side of the brain controls the left hand, effective thinkers should be able to utilise both left-handed and right-handed thinking by using their hands. If you are right-handed, how often do you use your left hand?

To effectively use both sides of your brain, try using the 'switching approach'. If you are left-handed, try switching to your right hand. If you are right-handed, switch to your left hand. If you use words to examine problems, switch to pictures. If you think visually, switch to words. If you are objective when it comes to solving problems, try using an approach that is more emotional. If thinking about a problem makes you very emotional, try to be more detached and see it as someone else's problem that does not affect you.

USING A WHOLE-BRAIN APPROACH

Using both sides of your brain is essential in order to think more creatively. As referenced previously in divergent and convergent thinking, using whole-brain thinking would be like viewing problems with a wide-angle lens and a telephoto lens. If you are more of a left-brain thinker, you need not abandon your logical and rational thinking but rather involve and avail yourself of the right hemisphere. If you are a right-brain thinker, you can become more balanced by involving more of the left hemisphere. Whole-brain thinking is when left-brain logic converges with right-brain perception.

When it comes to decision making, left-brain thinking is perhaps more prevalent. However, many a decision is made based on left-brain thinking coupled with our right-brain intuition. A decision that has already been made based on rationale and analysis can be influenced or even altered by one's insight, sixth sense or gut feeling.

Left- + Right-Brain Thinking = Whole-Brain Thinking

YOUR WHOLE-BRAIN QUOTIENT

Here's a simple exercise to evaluate your perception of your thinking preferences! On questions 1–10, circle the number in the scale that best describes you.

1. When working with data, are you ...
   Exacting   1 2 3 4 5 6 7 8 9 10   Informal

2. When making choices, do you ...
   Analyse   1 2 3 4 5 6 7 8 9 10   Jump in

3. Do you consider yourself more ...
   Predictable   1 2 3 4 5 6 7 8 9 10   Spontaneous

4. When living in the confines of rules, are you ...
   Within boundaries   1 2 3 4 5 6 7 8 9 10   Outside boundaries

5. When making decisions, are you ...
   Logical   1 2 3 4 5 6 7 8 9 10   Intuitive

6. When it comes to values, are you ...
   Rigid   1 2 3 4 5 6 7 8 9 10   Loose

7. When things go wrong, do you ...
   Criticise   1 2 3 4 5 6 7 8 9 10   Forgive

8. When it comes to living life, are you ...
   Intense   1 2 3 4 5 6 7 8 9 10   Light-hearted

9. Do you consider yourself more ...
   Close-minded   1 2 3 4 5 6 7 8 9 10   Open-minded

10. When it comes to getting what you want out of life,
    are you ...
    Negative   1 2 3 4 5 6 7 8 9 10   Positive

Interpret Your Score
Add up your score and identify your thinking skills according to your total score:

1–40	Your thinking style is left-brain-oriented.
41–50	Your thinking style is a balance between left- and right-brain thinking, although you are likely, depending on the situation, to have a tendency towards a left-brain approach.
51–60	Your thinking style is a balance between left- and right-brain thinking, although you are likely, depending on the situation, to have a tendency towards a right-brain approach.
61–100	Your thinking style is right-brain-oriented.

HELPING YOU AND YOUR TEAM TO THINK BETTER

Spend some time on specific thinking activities with your team – mind workouts – to induce a particular mode of thinking required for a given issue or situation.

SOLUTIONS Left Brain	IDEAS Right Brain

Because we live in a hurry-up society, we often settle for the first right answer instead of exploring a variety of ways to handle a situation. As a consequence, we look for a quick fix, which leads to a lack of alternatives. You can't afford not to invest the time needed to expand the thinking abilities of your team members.

When Mary started school, she came home every afternoon a happy and excited child. Her parents were elated. Then one afternoon, Mary returned home a very dejected and unhappy child. No amount of questioning led her parents to the reason why she was in this state. A few more days passed by before she finally opened up and blurted out, 'I'm stupid. Everybody laughed at me!' It turned out that the teacher had put a problem on the blackboard and asked the question, 'Which one of these is different?'

$$
\begin{array}{c|c}
a & b \\
\hline
c & d
\end{array}
$$

Mary answered the question by saying it was the 't'. She was the only one who had seen the 't' in the middle. Everybody else had identified one of the letters as being different.

There are a lot of problems and situations that have more than one right answer. We must not stop after we have found the first right answer. There may just be another answer that's even more 'right' for our situation.

Use right-brain thinking to generate as many ideas as possible, then switch to left-brain thinking to evaluate the ideas. This is a way of overcoming mental blocks that may prevent reaching the desired solution. Excessive left-brain thinking can overload your conscious mind with linear mental data that blocks your creative flow. Emptying your mind of linear data by using any of the right-brain exercises mentioned here will help you to maintain a balance between your right- and left-brain thinking.

Using mind workouts to stimulate thinking is the same as warming up before beginning any sports activity. You're the coach. You are getting your team members to practise some warm-up exercises so that they are ready to play the game and win! You are warming up their thinking processes so that they will formulate new ideas and solutions. Here are some simple and easy ways for your team members to warm up their thinking.

Ways to Induce Left-Brain Thinking
1. Solve a maths problem.
2. Connect the dots.
3. Plan the day.
4. Doodle in squares, oblongs and rectangles.
5. Take notes.
6. Work crossword puzzles.
7. Play board games.
8. Count.
9. Use words to solve a problem.
10. If left-handed, use the right hand.

Ways to Induce Right-Brain Thinking
1. Close eyes and listen to nature, music.
2. Work crossword puzzles.
3. Doodle in circles and patterns.
4. Daydream.
5. Solve riddles.
6. Draw.
7. Play word games.
8. Practise visualisation.
9. Use pictures instead of words to solve a problem
10. If right-handed, use the left hand.

Take the time to communicate to your team the reasons for doing brain warm-up exercises. The exercises will induce a particular type of thinking relative to a specific situation, problem or issue.

Prior to beginning the formal aspect of your meeting or planning session, spend 5 to 10 minutes involving your team members in the particular type of mind workout that will tap into the thinking approach you want to use. You would also be wise to involve your team in the planning of different activities to be used in meetings.

MIND WORKOUTS FOR TURBOCHARGED THINKING

Mind workouts stimulate the imagination and allow for flexibility in thinking! Structured thinking can limit your ability to see things in a different light. Mind workouts develop thinking, learning and memory capabilities for focus and improvement. Consider this example for a moment.

A porter at a major hotel was trying to locate the missing luggage of one of the guests. After a considerable length of time and despite the fact that this porter was extremely knowledgeable and hard-working, he was at a loss as to the location of the missing luggage. Had it not been for the guest's persistence in asking 'what if' over and over until the porter eventually found the luggage, it might never have been found.

The porter was a knowledgeable and intelligent person but had not practised thinking skills on a regular basis. So when he had to solve his customer's problem, he was hindered by his inability to be creative.

The porter was not inept or stupid. His example simply demonstrates that unless we use our thinking abilities every day, it is harder to find solutions or be creative. Many of us are apt to stop with one solution.

Thinking creatively is like any other skill – you learn by practising. The more you practise, the better you get. Here are some mind workouts for you to practise. These mind workouts will keep your thinking and your team members' thinking flexible.

⚡ Mind Workout – Word Game

Try this simple brain activity. Think of as many words as you can that begin with the letters CON.

_____	_____
_____	_____
_____	_____
_____	_____

⚡ Mind Workout – Making Decisions

When it comes to making a decision, fear can immobilise us. If you're not taking action in today's marketplace, your competition will simply pass you by. Here is a decision-making tool that will help you find alternatives.

In one minute, write down the problem and then list what you can control.

The Issue/Problem	What You Can Control

Mind Workout – Idea-Generating Questions

Questions can serve as a catalyst for possibilities. When you use questions such as these, look at the item or issue and then ask:

1. What else can it be used for (without any changes)?
2. What could be used instead? What else is like this?
3. How could it be adapted or modified for a new use?
4. What if it were larger (thicker, heavier, stronger)?
5. What if it were smaller (thinner, lighter, shorter)?

 Mind Workout – Problem Solving

Use the following three-column chart. In five minutes, list all team members' thoughts about a current issue in the first column, then do the same with the second and third columns.

'If Only'	'What Is'	'What Now?'

Mind Workout – In What Ways Might I (We)

This is a brainstorming technique to get your team members involved in problem solving and idea generation. Try these examples. Ask your team members the following:

In what ways might we improve customer service?

_____	_____
_____	_____
_____	_____
_____	_____
_____	_____

In what ways might we make our time more effective?

_____	_____
_____	_____
_____	_____
_____	_____
_____	_____

In what ways might we reduce downtime?

_____	_____
_____	_____
_____	_____
_____	_____

Here are a batch of word games that will help you and your team use divergent thinking. (Answers are below)

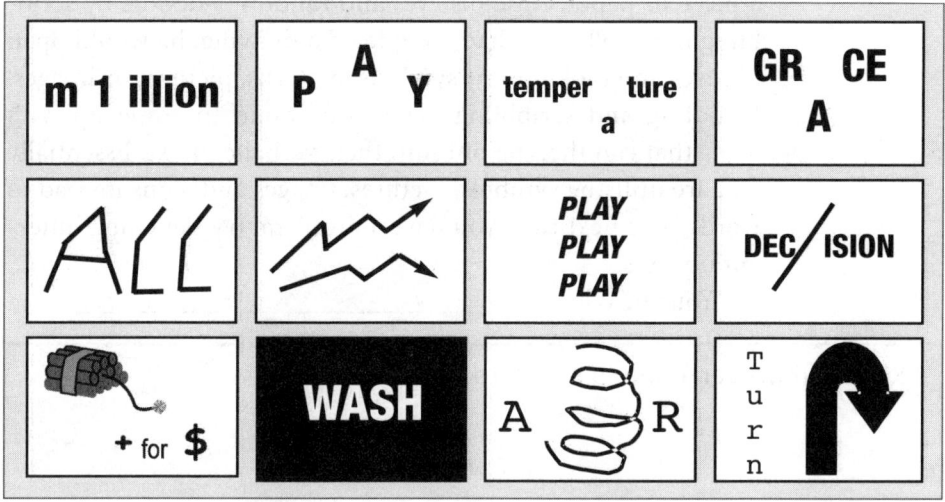

Answers:

one in a million	a raise in pay	a fall in temperature	fall from grace
all bent out of shape	ups and downs	triple play	split decision
more bang for your buck	whitewash	spring in the air	U turn

59

Mind Workout – Doodling and Scribbling

Leonardo da Vinci used doodling and scribbling as effective ways to stimulate thinking and idea generation. He would take a piece of paper, close his eyes and randomly doodle by scribbling lines. When he had completed a drawing, he would open his eyes and look for any symbols, patterns, pictures or images. Doodling and scribbling helps your mind to come up with ideas that can then be put into their verbal context. Essentially you are utilising symbols, pictures, images and icons instead of words. The next time you have a problem, try sketching different options.

Your problem is: _____

Sketch whatever images come to mind.

MIND WORKOUT – TAKE TIME TO THINK

Cultivate your imagination. Make a habit of spending three to five minutes a day concentrating on a simple object or form. Look at all of its characteristics. What aspects make it different from any other similar object? What aspects does it have that allow it to be functional? Make a point of using a different object every day. Ask yourself 'what if' questions. You may think that this is a useless activity, but you are allowing your subconscious mind to be able to concentrate in new and different ways, ways that you never would have thought possible. The more often you practise this activity, the more creative your thought process will become.

A story that encapsulates the essence of taking time to think follows. Henry Ford once hired an efficiency expert to examine the performance of the company. On completion of the report, which turned out to be most favourable, the expert had just one comment to make about one employee. The expert told Henry Ford, 'That lazy man sitting in the office over there has his feet on the desk every time I go by and appears to be wasting your money.' Henry Ford replied, 'That man over there came up with an idea once, with his feet planted right where they are now, that saved my company millions!'

Mind workouts are designed to stimulate your thinking and exercise your mental muscles. Don't let negative thinking interfere with your ability to practise these exercises, even though you may feel silly. Use visualisation, spontaneity and fantasy and have fun. Do not become judgemental or critical, but focus on creating something new and different. Take into account that practising the skill of thinking is the purpose of this book.

'The creative process does not end with an idea; it starts with one.'
Alex Osborn

CHAPTER FOUR

CREATING THE RIGHT ENVIRONMENT

Create the right kind of environment and capitalise on the talents and creative abilities of your team members. This is critical for achieving the four most important business outcomes: profits, productivity, employee retention and customer retention. These business outcomes translate into maximised shareholder value, increased market share, satisfied customers and improved performance. The challenge is how to build the right kind of work environment. You will need to define what creativity and innovation mean to your organisation and then fashion the appropriate climate. View this as an ongoing process.

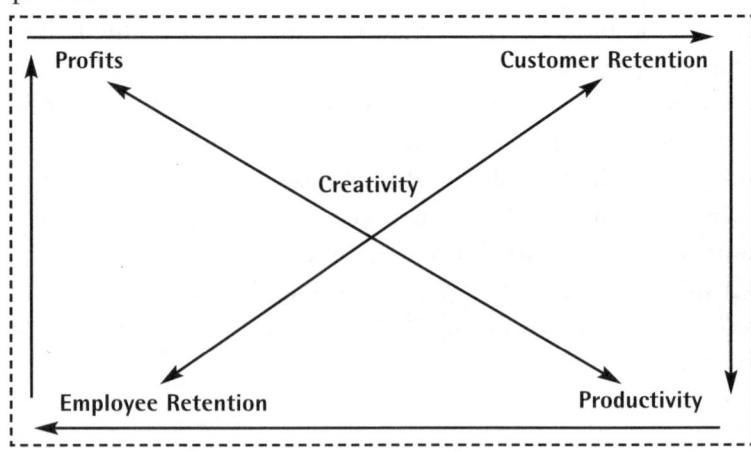

Corporate culture is a major component in driving an organisation. Corporate or company culture is a manifestation of how people think and feel. The way your team members behave, think and feel will have an impact on your organisation positively or negatively. Plainly, the physical environment influences the productivity of your team. Not so obvious is how the mental environment influences productivity. A company's infrastructure must match its business strategies. Creating an environment that is in keeping with your strategies is critical to achieving a 'creative culture' mindset.

'New ideas are not born in a conforming environment.' Roger von Oech

In the early 1900s when factories were more like sweatshops, Henry Heinz, founder of Heinz Foods, experienced bankruptcy. He decided some changes had to be made if his business was to succeed, and he notably developed a factory where workers enjoyed an environment that was conducive to higher productivity. Some of the benefits made available to them included free medical care, a library, piano music, and private lockers. These small changes made the employees feel valued, and the success of Heinz Foods continues today.

It is your responsibility to create an environment that will produce the support necessary to bring ideas to fruition. Consider the following physical environment components when creating an environment where your employees will be able to think and behave creatively.

THE PHYSICAL ENVIRONMENT

Environment influences behaviour more than is readily acknowledged. It's easier to be creative if you work in an environment where the energy flows. Look around your office. The physical layout of the work environment should support what you are trying to achieve.

Working in a drab office environment where there is no colour, no windows and stale air can be very depressing and can stifle creativity. The type of environment in which people work and live has a direct impact on productivity levels, happiness and health. This environment encompasses ergonomics, space, interior design, psychology, culture and sociology.

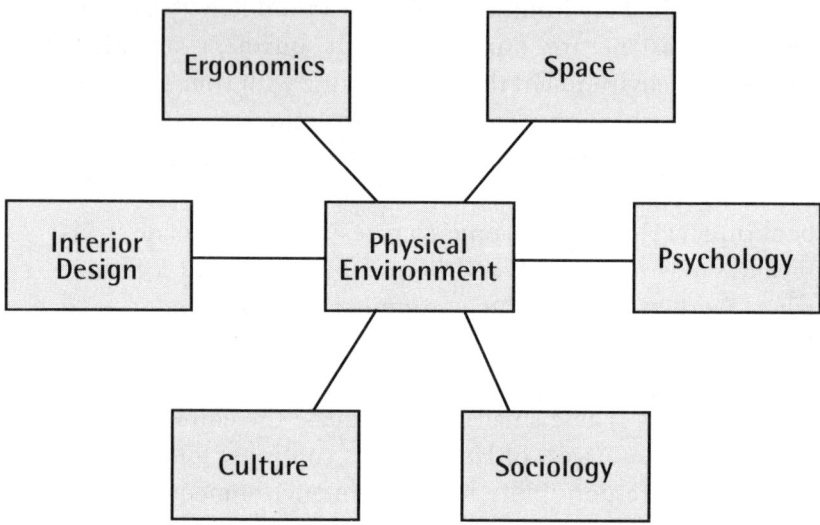

Changes to the environment are important! When things remain the same day after day, month after month, year after year, 'sameness' is reinforced within the organisation. This causes limitations in creative thinking. A familiar environment will reinforce familiar thoughts.

Anita Roddick, owner of The Body Shop, wants her people to 'fall in love' with change and is always changing the environment, thereby changing the atmosphere. 'Today's notice boards will be different from tomorrow's,' she says.

An organisation's work environment is both tangible and intangible. It has to be a place where creativity can take place.

Engage all of the senses – sight, sound, touch, smell and taste – to assist in breaking patterns that block creative thinking. Usually the environmental emphasis is on the visual aspect. It is important not to ignore the impact of the other four senses on both psychological and physical behaviours. Ultimately each of these five senses affects thoughts, feelings and actions.

SOUND

Music can provide stimulation and energy in the workplace, and enhance learning and productivity. You can improve the atmosphere just by adding music. The key is to select appropriate music and appropriate times when it is played. It is becoming commonplace in many organisations for radios or piped music to be played. There was a time when 'stuffy' banks would never have had music playing. That's changing!

An example of sound used in a creative form is Southwest Airlines. Flight attendants suddenly burst into song on take-offs, landings and sometimes in between, which makes the travel experience more fun.

Jan Carlzon, at Scandinavian Airlines headquarters, has created an environment designed to make people feel good and that stimulates and encourages them to do a better job. He even has had a string quartet play melodies at the lunch hour.

Anita Roddick has used sound very differently at The Body Shop. She believes that the aesthetics of an environment can act as a stimulant to her employees' imaginations. She has made the long corridors from her offices to her warehouses visually and musically stimulating. As employees walk down the corridors, they produce various sounds by pressing rubber suction cups and bamboo pipes that are attached to the walls. This is Roddick's way of keeping senses alive. By utilising the environment creatively, Roddick and her employees continue to innovate with momentum.

Music can have a profound effect on feelings and moods. Music can stimulate feelings of happiness or sadness, excitement or relaxation. The type of mood you want to create will determine your selection of music. Even if you are accustomed to silence, consider adding sound some of the time. It will change the tempo and will act as a stimulus in the work environment.

Certain sounds have also been recognised by doctors and health workers to have a beneficial effect on health.

SMELL – AIR AND AROMA

The sense of smell is a very important factor in being able to stir up emotions and memories. Think of a time when you experienced a happy emotion. You might have been on a seaside holiday with your family. Recreating that particular 'smell', namely the ocean, would evoke a happy memory. Similarly, if you lost your home and all of your belongings in a fire, the smell of wood smoke in the air might evoke a feeling of terror. To another person, wood smoke might bring up a happy memory of a romantic evening by the fire. A single scent can dredge up all kinds of emotions and enable you to relive memories.

So what does this have to do with a creative work environment? Air and aroma have a powerful effect. If you want to create the right kind of environment, the air plays an important part.

For example, you've probably heard about 'the sick-building syndrome'. This is an environment that is drab and cramped. There are very few windows, if any at all, and the air is stale.

An organisation needed to improve the performance and productivity of its 900 employees. Many causes of low morale and productivity were identified. One of the biggest problems was the work environment itself – break rooms, offices, corridors, rest rooms and cafeterias. In each of these areas, the air was the problem. The grey, dingy corridors consistently smelled like 'old, cooked cabbage'! This smell pervaded offices and employees' break rooms as well as other areas within the establishment. The rest rooms were neglected and infrequently cleaned. The solution was to change airflow in the air systems. In addition, the rest room cleaning schedules were drastically improved.

Minor issues are often overlooked, and yet their effects can have a major negative impact.

SIGHT – LIGHTING

In today's modern world, artificial lighting is the norm. It is a rare organisation that can use or rely on the natural source of sunlight. It is important, however, to know that light is one of the most powerful sources of creative energy.

Jane Wegscheider Hyman, author of *The Light Book*, says, 'Sunlight not only controls the circadian rhythm that determines your body's sleep-wake cycle, but it also strongly affects your appetite, mood, ability to heal and productivity. Sunlight plays an important role in your ability to be alert and your capacity for mental and physical tasks.' People living in climates where there is very little light are affected by seasonal affective disorder (SAD), an illness that causes mood changes, loss of concentration, lethargy, and alterations in thinking.

Overhead lighting that minimises shadows and brightly illuminates an area is necessary. Light bulbs that produce full-spectrum light duplicate the colour spectrum of natural light. 'Studies in artificial-light therapy,' according to Jane Hyman, 'have shown that people who were exposed to artificial lighting placed at eye level and were seated 3 feet away from the light for a period of two to six hours experienced a sense of calmness and alertness. They also experienced a surge of energy after 20 minutes. Their moods changed considerably to the point of feeling more sociable, cheerful and energetic.'

Consider taking breaks in the sunlight to regenerate energy, creativity and productivity. The right lighting conditions will make a huge difference in the work environment. It will induce more positive behaviours and increase creativity.

SIGHT – COLOURS

Colours influence people's attitudes and behaviours. Certain colours will affect people in different ways. Some colours can make people feel energised while others will be more calming. More than ever before, colour is being used to create specific environments.

The colours you incorporate into your environment should be selected so they inspire creativity.

Choose colours that will ignite the senses and feelings you want to infuse. According to Ron Gross, educational consultant, these examples of colour combinations will give you specific effects:

- Energetic: yellow/green, orange/white, green/purple, grey/red, blue/orange
- Dynamic: black/yellow, black/red, black/orange, red/orange, orange/blue
- Fresh: blue/white, yellow/green, green/light green, green/white, blue/grey

Some years ago, a study was conducted on the effects of colour in a workplace environment. The study included two environments and two groups. In the first environment, a group of people was subjected to working long hours over a period of one month in an environment where everything was grey including the office furniture. Grey, when used on its own, was one of the most negative colours. Participants said they felt depressed, lethargic and tired most of the time. The second group was placed in an environment of three separate colour combinations over a period of six weeks. Each separate session of colour exposure lasted two weeks. The results were startling compared to the first group. The behaviours of this second group were entirely opposite. Participants described senses and feelings that included excitement, energy, calmness and tranquillity.

If you have no control over the dominant colours in your work environment, be sure to include coloured items such as posters, paintings, vases or any of your personal items. They will still create an effect. The diversity of colours will stimulate the senses, thoughts and actions of those who spend a great deal of time in this environment.

TOUCH – TOOLS

Frequently changing the tools you use will help you and others to change thinking, solve problems and generate new ideas.

In an appropriate location such as a break room, lift, cafeteria or learning area, line the walls with white or coloured paper. Ask people to write their problems, ideas and solutions. Leave it up for a week. Ask all team members to contribute.

Display copies of letters from your customers in areas where employees can be reminded daily of how well they are doing.

'When all
you have is a
hammer,
everything
starts to look
like a nail.'
Abraham
Maslow

Create a 'wall of fame' or 'brag wall' where pictures, certificates of achievement and success articles can be displayed. This will show your team members how proud you are of them. It also lets them know that their contributions are important.

Consider using accomplishment as a tool. Before your team members leave for the day, spend 10 minutes sharing all the positive things that occurred that day. This is an excellent way to help your team members maintain high morale.

Ocean Basket, a successful seafood restaurant chain in South Africa, makes a practice of spending 45 minutes of each day with its team members discussing what went well or what went wrong, discussing how its customers feel and, most importantly, recognising excellence demonstrated by team members.

Hal Rosenbluth, CEO of Rosenbluth Travel, believes that the only way to continuously find solutions to problems is to have the kind of environment where spontaneity thrives. Every six months he sends out crayons and blank pieces of paper to employees to establish their current view of how they feel about the company. This is his way of measuring his organisation's 'happy quotient'. From the artwork he receives, he is able to establish what's really going on. A memo would not achieve the same feedback. This has been so successful that it has enabled him to revamp his organisation to make it a leading travel agency.

'What moves
men of
genius, or
rather what
inspires their
work, is not
new ideas,
but their
obsession
with the idea
that what
has already
been said is
still not
enough.'
Eugene
Delacroix

A large banking group was concerned that its employees did not communicate their good ideas as they thought of them. As a consequence, many good ideas were lost. To solve this problem, writing pads and pens were placed in strategic places, namely the company gym, locker rooms and even the company dining room. The thinking behind this was that employees generate good ideas when they are relaxed. Employees began to record ideas immediately because they had access to the tools. This practice paid off. One year later, the employees were in a completely different mindset.

LEADERS IN INNOVATION

Companies that are noted as leaders of innovation – 3M, Xerox, Bell Laboratories, Hallmark and Rubbermaid – make a conscious effort to inspire creativity.

NorthLight Studios, an innovative advertising agency, ensures that every meeting counts. Everyone who attends a meeting is expected to give at least two ideas for improvement in the areas of making money, reducing costs or making work more productive. By the end of the first year, NorthLight Studios increased productivity by 56 per cent!

Sony can be considered as one of the leaders in innovation. In an article in Continental Magazine, frequent contributor JoAnn Greco writes:

'In the mid 1940s, as countries around the world recovered from the effects and devastation of World War II, Japan emerged from the rubble along with many others and set about rebuilding its economy. Masaru Ibuka, a brilliant electronics engineer, along with his friend Akio Morita, a professor at the Tokyo Institute of Technology, established Tokyo Telecommunications Engineering Corporation. It was the summer of 1946, and the foundation had been laid for what was to become the Sony Corporation.

'It was evident from the beginning that innovation was a critical component for bringing out products that had never been made before. Sony is an excellent example of an organisation that is flexible and adaptable to changing direction at a moment's notice. They have determined that "adaptability" is their strength. At Sony, there is no discussion about failure but rather how often they succeed.

'Morita was responsible for conceiving the Walkman. His observation of the music-addicted kids whose boom boxes appeared to be glued to their bodies gave him the seed he needed for the creation of the Walkman.'

All of the above-noted companies are committed to creating an organisational environment that stimulates, inspires and supports innovation.

HUMOUR AND PLAY ENHANCE CREATIVITY

Do you ever wonder why children are so creative? They know how to play and have fun. Creativity requires playfulness, fun, humour and daydreaming. Researchers have found that fun and boisterous laughing are energy producing and can have the same effects as a 10-mile run! Laughter and humour are also beneficial for adjusting and reducing major life stresses. The most creative group environment is one where there is humour, spontaneity and fun. Attitudes change and people are more likely to get things done. Play is at the heart of creativity. Don't confuse play or fun with being childish.

Seriousness hinders the creative flow. Individuals who are too serious rarely come up with something new and exciting. Having a spirit of play loosens up the environment and allows people to be more open-minded. Humour and play can be the impetus that pushes your team into working together more creatively and collaboratively.

Quick question: Which of the following two companies will have employees open to possibilities and producing innovative solutions?

'If people did not some-times do silly things, nothing intelligent would ever get done.'
Ludwig Wittgenstein

Company X: Employees enjoy their work because they are having fun and are enthusiastic.

Company Y: Employees are not allowed any form of fun; their environment, therefore, is dreary, dull and tedious.

It's not hard to figure out which of the two is more creative. If you answered Company X, you're right!

Fun and play are often viewed negatively. Most adults have become too structured and logical in their thinking and consider play to be childish and silly. This negative view implies that people who play lack focus and are unproductive. Is it not true that we sometimes think people are 'goofing off' when we see them laughing? If you answered 'yes' to this question, perhaps it is time for you to change your view about play.

Teams that play well together will create results together. If disrupting the environment is a concern, consider establishing a 'play' room designated to creativity through play. Employees can use drawing boards, listen to music, play games, read or write. Decorate it so that it appears wacky and display it with jokes, posters and cartoons. Disney puts up whiteboard to allow people to write or draw their ideas for new characters of a story.

Robert Root-Bernstein, co-author of *Sparks of Genius*, says, 'Play returns us to the presymbolic drives of gut feelings, emotions, intuition and fun, from which creative insights stem, thereby making us inventors. When rules-bound work doesn't yield the insights or results we want to achieve, when conventional thought, behaviour and disciplinary knowledge become barriers to our goals, play provides a fun and risk-free means of seeing from a fresh perspective, learning without constraint, exploring without fear.'

Creativity takes a lot of hard work and discipline. Humour and fun loosen up both the atmosphere and the people and

'Almost all new ideas have a certain aspect of foolishness when they are first produced.'
Alfred North Whitehead

enhance creativity. To make this point, research was conducted by an organisation to assess the role humour played and what difference it made to its employees' productivity.

Participants were divided into two groups. One group had to sit quietly in a room for two hours. The other group was in another room listening to humorous tapes and laughter, also for a period of two hours. Each group was then given a series of problems to solve. The group that had been subjected to two hours of humour came up with many creative solutions. The group that had received no stimulation struggled to come up with any solutions.

It is to your benefit to encourage your employees to have fun. Humour encourages creative thinking by providing an environment where people can be more creative. Without fun, it is easy to slip into a state of exhaustion and even depression. Fun is necessary. An environment where fun is allowed and encouraged will have people who are energised, positive and more creative.

> 'People do not quit playing because they grow old. They grow old because they quit playing.'
> Oliver Wendell Holmes

Southwest Airlines uses humour in most of its in-flight announcements, thus creating a fun atmosphere for both the employees and passengers. This makes even the most intolerable travel pleasurable.

Apple Computers calls its break rooms Oz and Toto, to remind people that there is a wizard in everyone. Calling the computer Gronk makes it seem more user-friendly than the Deck10A30.

Ben & Jerry's Ice Cream created a 'joy gang' – a team of people with the task of finding ways to put fun back into work. One of the team's biggest successes was 'Elvis Day' when all employees arrived at work dressed up as the 'King'! Co-founder Jerry Greenfield says, 'Things at work are tough. With all the tasks we have to perform and the stress people have, we want to infuse our workplace with joy.'

Another company that encourages fun in the workplace is Microsoft. Employees play miniature golf in the corridors. Elevators are used to move the ball from the tee on the first floor to the green on the second floor. Microsoft's managers have a 'morale budget'. They are empowered to spend this budget on fun in any way they see fit. For Microsoft, fun induces a sense of relaxation, which gets things done and ensures momentum.

Virgin Atlantic Airways is an ideal example of creativity in motion. According to CEO Richard Branson, Virgin Airlines is in the entertainment business … at 25,000 feet. While other airlines compete by cutting fares, Branson maintains fares and focuses on providing exceptional service, including in-flight massages, exercise facilities, showers and movies. Transportation is merely the mode of entertainment.

What are you currently doing to create a fun, playful environment for your team? Consider letting team members be less serious on certain days of the year. You can do this by having 'theme'-dress days, wearing costumes or masks, playing games, hosting monthly lunches with a jester, or setting out challenge courses with fun awards. Appoint a 'fun committee' whose sole objective is to ensure a workplace environment where creativity can thrive.

> 'The debt we owe to the play of imagination is incalculable.'
> Jung

> 'Where all men think alike, no one thinks very much.'
> Walter Lippmann

What Elements Can You Change to Enliven Your Environment?

1. Describe how your ideal environment would look.
   _____
   _____

2. If you were to install music and sound, what would be most conducive for your unique environment?
   _____
   _____

3. What would you do to make use of humour and play?
   _____
   _____

4. List the ideas that most appeal to you from this chapter.
   _____
   _____

5. What are the benefits to you and your team members for changing your work environment?
   _____
   _____

6. When will you begin making changes?
   _____
   _____

7. Which area will you begin with?
   _____
   _____

8. List any other ideas.
   _____
   _____

CHAPTER FIVE

UNDERSTANDING AND APPLYING BASIC PRINCIPLES OF CREATIVITY

Innovation is the lifeblood of any organisation and ultimately represents the most important sustainable competitive advantage. Without it, there would be very little progress and the same patterns would be forever repeated. Organisations just can't stay alive and moving forward without creative thinking and ideas.

The word 'create' is derived from the Latin word 'creare,' which means to produce, cause to grow, have to come into existence. Everyone has creative ability, more even than they actually use. When you think about it, everything that has ever been invented began as an idea! People create what they imagine, and everybody has imagination. The key is to learn how to use imagination and open your mind to your creative ability.

Dr JP Guilford, a psychologist, and E Paul Torrance, a researcher, found that young children are generally more creative than adults. They found that children 5 years old and younger have original responses 90 per cent of the time. These creative responses drop to 7 per cent by the time a child is 7 years old. The original responses further decline to 2 per cent by the time children become adults!

The more you engage in creative thinking, the better you will become at it. You will be able to solve problems more easily, remember better and produce even more ideas!

> 'Imagination is more important than knowledge. Knowledge is limited, imagination embraces the world, stimulating progress, giving birth to evolution.'
> Albert Einstein

Much of creativity is the ability to see something different-ly. Taking an idea or a concept and putting it into a different context can give it a different meaning.

Coco Chanel was able to take the fashion industry and mould it into something completely new and different. Chanel's approach to fashion was based on her life philosophy that for 'everything she did not like, there was an opposite that would be far more preferable'. She used her creativity to 'fashion' the fashion industry by breaking the rules and creating something entirely new.

The act of brainstorming and the use of imagination allow us to reconstruct or rework information to formulate new plans and goals. Brainstorming generates numerous ideas and options in a very short space of time. Guilford and Torrance, well-known for their studies in creative thinking, identified five key creative abilities in the brainstorming process.

1. **Fluency** – the volume of ideas generated in total. Making lists is one way of increasing fluency. If you are doing this as a team activity, look for at least 20 ideas from a novice group and 30 from experienced thinkers.

2. **Flexibility** – the number of category areas. Flexibility is the diversity of ideas generated. Flexibility is the ability to see beyond the ordinary.

3. **Originality** – the ability to be able to generate unique and uncommon ideas. For example, take an ordinary paper clip and brainstorm new and unusual uses for it. One of the very first ideas that is usually stated is a utility-type hook! Originality would be a doctor's needle.

4. **Elaboration** – the ability to be able to add, change or elim-inate any part of the item. It is the number of details added onto the idea. Example: Make the paper clip into a fly for luring fish by combining it with a feather.

5. **Judging** – the last step. Evaluate the ideas for possible and practical applications.

 Mind Workout – The Paper Clip

In one minute, write down as many uses as possible for a paper clip. This mind workout illustrates divergent thinking. Before you begin, remember to use the following guidelines for effective idea generation.

Guidelines
- Go for quantity of ideas and not quality of ideas.
- Don't evaluate; defer judgement.
- Go for radical ideas.
- Think in pictures to find more possibilities.
- Build on existing ideas.
- Have fun.

How did you do? Did your ideas incorporate all five abilities? Were you able to utilise the full minute or did you run out of ideas? If you didn't do as well as you hoped, don't be discouraged. You have started thinking differently. This is the first step towards successful creativity.

An activity like this is an excellent warm-up technique to use with your team before a brainstorming session.

🗲 Mind Workout – Flexibility

Flexibility is essential for creating numerous ideas. You can develop flexible thinking by using the skill of association. You can do this by finding a connection among seemingly dissimilar words using Mednick's Remote Associates Test (1962).

For each set of three words, your objective is to find an associated word that all three have in common. For example, the words 'wheel', 'electric' and 'high' can all be paired with 'chair'.

Example

chorus	bee	side	_line_
chorus line	*beeline*	*sideline*	

1. surprise	line	birthday	_____
2. mark	shelf	telephone	_____
3. stick	maker	tennis	_____
4. blue	cottage	cloth	_____
5. motion	poke	down	_____
6. gem	wall	stepping	_____
7. piggy	green	lash	_____
8. lunch	car	gift	_____
9. foul	ground	pen	_____

Don't be discouraged if you found this hard. Remember that we learn by doing. Were you an expert when you first began using a computer? No! You practised and followed instructions. Now you can hardly remember what it was like not to be able to use a computer!

As you begin to use your creative-thinking abilities more and more, you will find that the creative process becomes easier and easier. The time will come when you are adept at creative thinking.

WHAT IS CREATIVITY?

There are various definitions for 'creativity'. Experts define creative thinking as 'being able to think in divergent modes to arrive at finding a new and original thought and departing from either the conventional or usual in idea'.

Joseph V Anderson, professor of marketing at Rollins College, defines creativity: 'That which makes things, that which combines things, and that which changes things.' Anderson states, 'It is the act of making something out of nothing.'

Perhaps the most imaginative definition of creativity is Rosabeth Moss Kanter's version as quoted in 'Creating the Creative Environment' in the *Management Review* of February 1986. She says, 'The overall key to creativity is what I have come to call "kaleidoscope thinking". The kaleidoscope is a wonderful metaphor for the creative process because the gadget allows us to twist reality into new patterns. In a kaleidoscope, a set of fragments form a pattern but aren't locked into place. All you have to do is shake it, twist it, change angle, change perspective, and the exact same fragments form an entirely new pattern. Reality, the kaleidoscope tells us, is only a temporary arrangement. Creativity consists of rearranging the pieces to create a new reality.'

Another completely different angle to the definition of creativity is that of Edward de Bono, author of *de Bono's Thinking Course* and inventor of the term 'lateral thinking'. He believes the word 'creativity' to be inadequate. He states: 'A creative person may have a way of looking at the world which is different from the way other people see the world, but if the person is locked in their own special perception, unable to change perception or see the world in another way, the creative person is actually "rigid" at the same time. Although in no way does it diminish their value to society, neither does it diminish their ability to create within their special perception.'

What is interesting about de Bono's theory of 'lateral thinking' is the ability to change perception and to keep on changing perception. He defines 'lateral thinking' as pattern switching within a patterning system. Working within existing patterns will not itself lead to new patterns. So, in ordinary terms, de Bono gives this description: 'Grandma is knitting, and young Susie is disturbing Grandma by playing with the ball of wool. The father suggests putting Susie in the playpen. The mother suggests that it might make more sense to put Grandma in the playpen. Definitely, a different way of looking at things which is quite logical in hindsight.'

Whichever way you define creativity, you will know you are thinking creatively when you are able to easily come up with many options and different ways of doing things.

Find out what creativity means to you by answering the following questions on the next page.

> 'Once a new idea springs into existence, it cannot be unthought. There is a sense of immortality in a new idea.'
> Edward de Bono

The Meaning of Creativity

1. What is your definition of creativity?

   _____

   _____

   _____

2. How can you use creative thinking in your life?

   _____

   _____

   _____

3. When was the last time you used your creative abilities?

   _____

   _____

   _____

4. What are your expectations of your employees when it comes to creative thinking?

   _____

   _____

   _____

5. Do you provide your employees with the necessary tools to be creative?

   _____

   _____

   _____

6. What do you need to do differently? What action can you take today to make improvements in your thinking and in that of your team?

   _____

   _____

   _____

UNDERSTANDING THE CREATIVE PROCESS

For many years, researchers and scientists have studied the processes required for being creative. In 1945, Graham Wallas, an American psychologist, identified the four stages of the creative process, which he discussed in his book *The Art of Thought*.

1. **Preparation – Getting Ready**

    The first part of being creative involves the collection of information and the gathering of data. In the preparation process, you will have to prompt your imagination. You do this by reading, researching and reviewing information. You might also talk with and interview people who may have more insight. You may even find that talking with someone who is detached from the situation will give you a non-biased viewpoint.

2. **Incubation – Thinking About It**

    The incubation stage is more commonly known as the time-out phase. This is when you stop focusing on the issue or problem at a conscious level. You allow time for your subconscious mind to generate more ideas and solutions to a given situation.

    Your best ideas are probably not going to come at the exact time you would prefer or when you are expecting them. You know this only too well! Ideas emerge over time. Sometimes, taking a break is the key to creativity.

    Intensity overloads your brain. Thinking occasionally about the problem, without pressure, is a better approach. Incubation is the period in which the subconscious processes of the mind take hold and are able to formulate solutions or winning ideas. Whatever you do, don't think of this as a waste of time. Taking time out is a vital component of reaching solutions. In the midst of problem solving, it is necessary to relax. It is important to realise that the incubation stage is occurring at the subconscious level. Therefore, you must let go and let your mind process the information at its own pace.

Very often the answer to your problem is in your subconscious. Unless you allow the incubation period to occur, you will have a hard time achieving a revelation. If you have done the preparation by thinking extensively about the problem and then letting go, ideas for solutions will come and usually at a time when you least expect them. Incubation will more often than not produce the right answer at the right time! As an example, look at Ben Franklin. He discovered electricity while flying a kite in a thunderstorm. A lot of people would think he was ridiculous to fly a kite at a time like that, yet taking time out was the very foundation of his genius.

3. **Illumination – Aha!**

The illumination stage is when you reach a point that is best known as the 'aha' or the 'eureka' stage. It's when the inspiration or revelation seemingly comes from out of the blue. It will often occur at a time that is totally unrelated to anything that you may be doing.

The great thinker of ancient Greece, Archimedes, was a mathematician and physicist when he came upon his 'bathtub' realisation. Legend has it that King Hiero of Syracuse gave a golden crown to Archimedes, who was an adviser to the king. Archimedes was to test the crown for purity without damaging it. The king suspected it contained some lead and base metal and was not made entirely of gold as he had commissioned. Archimedes considered the problem for some time and eventually determined a way of testing it. The solution suddenly came to him when he noticed how the water level rose when he got in the bath. A given volume of gold was heavier than the same volume of silver; therefore, a given mass of gold, when placed in water, would displace more than the same mass of silver. The same mass of a mixture of the two would displace something in between. When he discovered that he could test the purity of gold, he jumped out of the bath yelling 'Eureka! Eureka!' meaning 'I have found it!'

Similarly this kind of revelation may happen to you when you are exercising, shopping, driving, taking a shower, watching a movie, or engaging in any other pastime. What's really happening is that the new ideas are passing from the subconscious level of the mind to the conscious level of the mind. The illumination stage can be a result of applied conscious effort or may come spontaneously. It is also the stage where intuition and insight play a significant part in creating solutions.

Allow a reasonable amount of time in your life for relaxation or downtime. Allowing yourself a time-out from the problem allows your subconscious to process the information that it already has stored. That is why ideas come to you at the most peculiar times and when you are involved in totally unrelated activities. It is important to avoid any evaluation at this point.

4. Verification – Checking It Out

Finally, the verification stage occurs when the idea has arrived from the mind's subconscious level, and you have the 'seed' of an idea. You don't have the complete plan or strategy yet. You plant your 'idea seed' the same as a seed in a garden. Then you supply the necessary nutrients – your knowledge and expertise – to allow it to grow and reach a solution. At this point, you evaluate your idea for its feasibility and functionality, utilise the resources you have available to you, and take the necessary action.

Used in its entirety, this four-stage creative process is whole-brain thinking. It is using both subconscious and conscious processes. The incubation and illumination stages involve subconscious thinking processes. The first stage, preparation, and the last stage, verification, are well-defined conscious tasks.

When you begin using this four-step methodology for creativity, it is imperative that each of the steps is practised separately and in sequence. Allow time between each step for your subconscious and conscious to work together to achieve the desired result! Many individuals expect instant results and are not prepared to wait. Idea generation and finding solutions don't happen that way! If you want results, then you must be prepared to allow a certain amount of time between each step for the whole thinking process to work.

Applied Thinking + Imagination = Creative Thinking

To use these four steps effectively, begin with the following

Applied-Thinking Approach

1. Write a statement of the problem.

_____

_____

_____

2. What is the current situation?

_____

_____

_____

3. What are the consequences if the situation continues?

_____

_____

_____

4. What steps will you take to gather the appropriate information?

_____

_____

_____

5. What is the desired outcome?

_____

_____

_____

Take a break and just let the ideas come!

Once you have answered these five questions, it is essential that each of the four steps – preparation, incubation, illumination and verification – is kept distinctly separate. Again, be sure to allow a period of time between each of the four steps for this applied-thinking approach to work. Be sure to use the different thinking tools that have been shared with you throughout this book. Change context and tempo by using music, fun and activities.

TAPPING INTO YOUR CREATIVITY

Fundamentally, we are all creative. The question is, 'How do we use our creative abilities to our best advantage?' The best way to tap into our creativity is through flexibility of thinking and practise, practise, practise. Tapping into creativity means letting go of any preconceived ideas and developing ways to unleash our thinking. The following three steps will help you do this. As a leader, this will help you to cultivate and develop your team members' core talents.

1. **Recognise that creativity is abundant, if you are aware.**
   Make a conscious effort to be aware of what you do and all that is around you.

   Typically, we ride to work the same way day after day, often ignoring what we see around us because it is so routine. Our surroundings, however, can be a source of inspiration, revelation and insight for our thinking processes.

   Develop the habit of watching. Start paying attention and noticing people, objects and nature around you. For example, when you see a young mother crossing the street with a baby in the stroller, note what you see. Does the mother look happy or sad? Is the baby sleeping or awake?

   Take time to really look at nature. When you pass a tree,

> 'The average human being looks without seeing, listens without hearing, touches without feeling, eats without tasting, moves without physical awareness, inhales without awareness of odour or fragrance and talks without thinking.'
> Leonardo da Vinci

notice what kind of tree it is. Are the leaves green? Or are they turning brown, making way for winter? Look at the shadows and take note of their flickering movements. When you are listening to classical music on the radio, visualise how each instrumentalist looks. Imagine that the people you see in the street are all dancing to the tune you are hearing.

Develop your curiosity. Remember, curiosity is an important component of awareness and thinking creatively. When you were a child, you were curious and you saw so much wonder in the world. Curiosity helped Bill Gates create Microsoft. It helped Archimedes discover the law of displacement. It helped Maria Montessori transform childhood education, and helped Newton discover the law of gravity. Einstein once said, 'I know quite certainly that I have no special gift except that I have curiosity, obsession and dogged endurance which, combined with self-critique, have brought me ideas.'

Action Planning

What three actions can you take to help your team develop its awareness?

1. _____

_____

2. _____

_____

3. _____

_____

2. **Affirm to yourself that you are creative in order to overcome the fears that inhibit creativity.**

Creative people believe they are creative. People who think they are not creative actually talk themselves into not being creative. They say, 'I'm just not creative!' This statement in itself is an inhibitor. What you believe to be true usually becomes true. Your mind creates what you programme it to create. Therefore, you must remember that some of the most important words you will ever say are the words you say to yourself. Affirmations help you to programme your thinking.

An affirmation is a personal and positive statement said in the present tense: I am creative, I am coming up with new ideas, I use my creative talents, or I am finding ways to solve problems. An affirmation enables you to internalise something through constant repetition. It causes your subconscious mind to act accordingly. It is important to affirm that you are creative in order to influence your own thinking and change your beliefs. You may never be a Marie Curie or a Leonardo da Vinci, but the ideas you contribute are necessary and important.

Mark Victor Hansen and Jack Canfield, New York Times best-selling authors of the famous *Chicken Soup for the Soul* books, bear testimony to this. When they decided to write a book, they decided it had to be a 'megabestseller' not just a book. Every night when they went to sleep they rehearsed in their minds, independently of each other, 'megabest-selling title, megabest-selling title'. Because they wanted a perfect title for their book, they would repeat this affirmation at least 400 times. They even went so far as to affirm that the perfect title would come to one of them in the middle of the night. According to Mark Victor Hansen:

> 'Affirmations are like prescriptions for certain aspects of yourself that you want to change.'
> Jerry Frankhauser

'Jack got it. He woke up, got goosebumps and said, "*Chicken Soup for the Soul*"! He called me in the middle of the night and we had the title.' Today Mark Victor Hansen and Jack Canfield are millionaires. Affirmations … do they work? It appears they do!

In a 1997 movie entitled 'The Edge,' starring Anthony Hopkins and Alec Baldwin, a man-eating bear terrorises their characters after their plane crashes in a remote and treacherous mountainous area. To survive, they must 'kill the bear', but they have no weapons! Anthony Hopkins, who plays the part of a billionaire, recalls how 11-year-old boys killed lions in Africa by using primitive weapons and playing the lions at their own game. With this in mind, he ultimately convinces Alec Baldwin's character that it can be done. Alec Baldwin plays the 'naysayer'. He complains, 'It can't be done. We don't have weapons. We're going to die', and he refuses to even attempt to kill the bear. In a heated scene, Anthony Hopkins yells, 'I'm going to kill the bear.' He insists that Alec Baldwin repeat this statement over and over, 'I'm going to kill the bear. I'm going to kill the bear.' Anthony Hopkins then has his uncooperative fellow survivor scream, 'What one man can do, another man can do. What one man can do, another man can do.' Finally, Anthony Hopkins takes Alec Baldwin into the present moment yelling, 'Today, I'm going to kill the bear.' The bear is killed.

Although only a movie, it carries a powerful message. Anthony Hopkins' character simply used 'affirmations' to get Alec Baldwin's character to reprogramme his thinking into believing he could kill the bear.

Our thoughts have power! Our thinking influences our feelings and shapes our behaviours. Affirmations help us take control of our thoughts and achieve positive outcomes. The belief that you are creative can be achieved through positive affirmation.

> ⚡ Write your own creative affirmation:
>
> _____
>
> _____
>
> _____
>
> _____
>
> _____
>
> _____

3. **Purposefully and systematically develop your creative abilities.**

Learn and practise thinking skills and problem-solving processes. Enormous amounts of knowledge can be gained through observation and a questioning attitude. Think back to a time when you were a child. Which words did you use most often? They were probably 'look' and 'why'. As you grew older, you may have been discouraged from inquiry. And as adults, you may not want to 'rock the boat', preferring to 'let sleeping dogs lie' and refraining from asking too many questions.

An inquisitive approach to everything you do stretches your mind. A questioning attitude will help you develop your ability to conceptualise.

Try answering these eight simple questions with someone you know.

> 'Learning is movement from moment to moment.'
> J. Krishnamurti

1. Why is a marshmallow soft?
2. Why are clouds suspended in midair?
3. Why do we get older?
4. Before earth was created, what was there?
5. Why do we eat?
6. What is happiness?
7. How does the colour purple taste?
8. Why do trees move?

What three practices will you utilise to begin developing your creative abilities?

1. _____
   _____
   _____
   _____

2. _____
   _____
   _____
   _____

3. _____
   _____
   _____
   _____

CHAPTER SIX

BUILDING A CREATIVE ORGANISATION

Building a creative organisation involves changing the status quo, which can be difficult and uncomfortable. Change is a condition for creativity and growth. Change brings opportunity. Yet your team members are likely to resist change, as it takes them out of their comfort zones. When you have appropriately planned for it and you understand that there may be resistance to it, you are ready to manage the change.

> 'A competitive world has two possibilities for you. You can lose. Or, if you want to win, you can change.'
> Lester C. Thurow

To build a creative organisation, you need to determine ahead of time how you will handle the change and how you will prepare your team. When there is resistance, there is a need to understand why that resistance exists. There are times during change when employees don't buy in or make productive contributions to the change. This results in employees sabotaging the change and creating chaos. This is both costly and time-consuming.

For the change to work, your team members need to have positive perspectives. It is not going to be the process, the system or the technology that brings about failure during change. It will be the people. Human beings are uncomfortable with uncertainty and are comfortable with certainty! Very often there is a stubborn refusal to adapt to changing circumstances. People insist on doing things the old way. When this happens, it can produce stagnation and limit growth. They will also have a tendency to resist anything that requires effort. Given the choice of doing something that requires little effort or doing something that is difficult, most people will opt for easy.

What it ultimately comes down to is that people can be obstacles to the implementation of the change. If they don't support it or if there is doubt and confusion, how can it possibly work? There has to be willingness and acceptance by your team members. Their attitudes are a key factor to your success in building a creative organisation.

BECOME A MASTER OF CHANGE

You will have to become the force of change in order to remain competitive in increasingly aggressive markets. This means continuously adapting to an unpredictable future and rapid change, so aptly described as 'a blurred economy' by futurists Stan Davis and Chris Meyer. Success will come from how quickly you respond to changes.

'If we want things to stay as they are, things will have to change.'
Guiseppe Tomasi di Lampedusa

You can have all the necessary traits required to be an effective leader, but if you are unable to manage and handle change effectively, your opportunity for success can be severely hindered.

The pursuit of change should be a constant management priority. If your business isn't changing continually, something is wrong! In this day and age, change is just about the only constant. To resist it is sheer madness. Change is inevitable, change is growth.

C reates

H uge

A nd

N ever-ending

G rowth

E xperiences

Some changes are difficult. Others are natural and relatively easy. The leader's perspective about change affects the team members positively or negatively. If you are to create a company where your team members are consistently thinking creatively, your goal must be to develop your team members so that change-oriented thinking becomes a habit for everyone. Winning often depends on your change strategy. All too frequently change initiatives fail because the change is not given priority and the approach used is ineffective.

No matter whether you have instigated the change or it has been instigated by an external factor, managing the change can be stressful for you and your team members. Being cognisant of this and strategically planning the change are critical to a successful outcome. If you don't do this, your team members will become resistant and cause the change to fail.

Resistance to new ideas is common and kills creativity, excitement and motivation. As a leader, you can't play the change game alone. Your team members need to support the changes you make. Therefore, finding ways to build up their support is critical to ensure victory. Your greatest challenge is to overcome the barriers to change. To do this, you must first detect and then understand the reasons for the resistance. Great leaders go one step further by finding out and understanding the individual reasons for resistance. Different people will be resistant for different reasons.

> 'You can and should shape your own future. Because if you don't, someone else surely will.'
> Joel Barker

UNDERSTANDING RESISTANCE

Change brings about a continuous state of evolution that very often threatens the way we see the world. The 'way we see' something is the 'way it is'. It's a matter of perception. Like the half-glass of water: Is the glass half-empty or half-full?

When the 'way we see' is threatened, we can be resistant to seeing things differently. We all have a frame of reference through which we interpret what we experience in life. Simply put, this is our 'perceptive filter'. This 'filter' radically affects our thinking and judgement to the point that new, incoming ideas are likely to be rejected. Author William G Dyer tells us: 'People do not change easily or all at once. Most of us need a chance to try out new ways and become familiar with new procedures.'

As you build a culture of highly creative-thinking individuals, you bring change that takes people out of their comfort zones. New ideas cause change, which ultimately creates uncertainty and often more work. Your job will be to change the mindsets that prevail in the workplace. This takes understanding and time.

You will need to find ways to change perceptions or, to use a more scientific term, change 'paradigms'. A paradigm is a model of reference and the foundation on which we form our beliefs. Beliefs influence thoughts, which in turn influence behaviours. Changing paradigms can be very difficult, as people try to hold on to the way things are no matter what.

New ideas can undergo a lot of conflict before they are widely accepted. Some of our greatest thinkers in history, who dared to discover new things and make public their findings, had to tolerate ridicule and contempt from people who refused a new way of thinking. Galileo was placed under house arrest for supposed heresy. Darwin's name is still embroiled in controversy more than a century later.

Going back centuries when the world was perceived to be flat, there was tremendous resistance when the paradigm shifted to the world being round. The paradigm was further shifted by Copernicus' theory, which was in direct contrast to Ptolemy's theory that the earth was the centre of the universe. There was such resistance that his theory was considered heresy.

There are so many examples of outstanding people who have changed the world dramatically by breaking with tradition. They have met resistance simply because people did not want change and wished to maintain the status quo. This, too, can happen in your organisation.

A more recent example is the layout of the typewriter keys, 'QWERTY'. More than 100 years ago, the keys were designed this way to prevent typists from jamming the keys. Still today, with the advancements in technology, the keyboards on electronic equipment and computers are the same despite the fact that the jamming of the keys no longer applies. In fact, there are many efficient layouts that would permit faster typing!

Fixed paradigms can severely impede success. Therefore, changing these paradigms is essential to building a culture of creative-thinking team members. No amount of wishing for things to return to the way they used to be will bring them back. Help your team members change the way they think in order to change existing paradigms that are limiting progress.

Having an effective approach to managing change will be more effective.

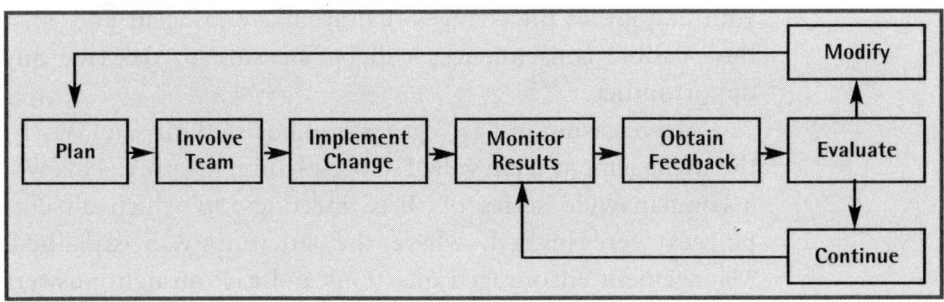

LEADING THE WAY TO MAKE EFFECTIVE CHANGES

Communicating Change

Good communication can minimise resistance. The way in which you communicate a change to your employees will make a huge difference in how change is either accepted or resisted. A poor approach to take when change is occurring is to speak in generalities. Even worse is not to communicate at all! Rumours will escalate and the consequence will be the 'grapevine'! Grapevines usually distort the truth, and once the rumour is out there, it's very difficult to reverse it.

Communicating change sometimes means breaking bad news to people. Bad news is bad news, and it cannot be forever concealed. It is only fair to communicate the facts as soon as possible. The sooner, the better.

There are times when you are not in a position to give out much information. Even so, as a leader it is important to communicate this by saying, 'All right, this is the situation. I don't have the words you want to hear, but we've got a couple of choices. Either we resist the change and hold on to the way things are, or we get involved and see how we can influence the change positively for ourselves.' As best you can, describe to your employees the changes that are likely to occur and what the possible consequences will be. Be sure to describe any opportunities.

A large casino in Las Vegas was to be listed for sale. Wisely, the management team called a 'big-picture' meeting. This was a companywide series of three meetings, to which all employees were invited, where the situation was explained. Management encouraged questions and gave straight answers with no punches being pulled! Thereafter, a series of department meetings was held to discuss specific changes and the impact on each department. The resistance to the change was limited because employees understood the reasons for the change and how it would affect them.

Involving Team Members

Change implementation requires involvement from all members of the team. Involve everyone in one way or another. When you just give orders without asking for employee input, team members don't feel as though they are a part of the programme and will likely resist. Input and involvement create ownership. Ownership will motivate them to work harder to make the change work. Where possible, make sure that you involve your employees in the planning stages of the change. This will minimise the chance of problems surfacing later. Set up small task teams to deal with certain areas of the plan or handle issues that may arise.

Giving the Benefits

It's not difficult to understand that, during times of change, an employee's first thought might be, 'What will happen to my job?' or 'Will I keep my job?' If employees feel threatened, they will resist, because they see no benefit for themselves. No workers have ever been motivated by any kind of change that is going to benefit stockholders at their expense. Let's be realistic! It is perfectly normal to respond to any kind of change from your own perspective and self-interest. People will judge change according to how it personally benefits or threatens them. If you don't take the time to explain what's in it for them, you can be sure that resistance will prevail. Stress how the change will improve their chances of realising their individual potential. Support your plan with facts and statistics. Explain market demands, customer perceptions and competitive trends. Help them to visualise a positive outcome and ensure that they understand the negative consequences of not making the changes. If people know and understand the reasons for the change and the benefits to them, they are likely to handle the change with greater enthusiasm and sense of direction.

Seeking Feedback
Feedback is a powerful tool during change. Seek feedback to make sure that the change has been correctly interpreted. When obtaining feedback, you will get positive opinions as well as negative ones. These cannot be ignored. If handled correctly, feedback will contribute to the planning process. You may receive information that you hadn't considered, which will help the change take place more smoothly. Feedback also will give you information you need to identify and assess whether your goals are being met.

Avoiding Pitfalls
When faced with obstructive ringleaders who will not reform, you have two things you can do: convert them or find a way to remove them. Resistance will come in the form of either active or passive resistance and will occur for different reasons. Understanding the reasons is essential.

Building Confidence
The job of neutralising resistance to change requires that you help people believe in themselves. It is important to help them believe that they can manage the change without failing. If employees believe that they do not have the right skills and knowledge, their confidence levels fade and resistance levels rise. Help build their confidence by emphasising their strengths and increasing their knowledge and skill base. Help them to

take one step at a time by showing them what they can do instead of what they can't do.

Monitoring Progress

As a change project advances, monitor morale closely and be sure to act quickly if it begins to deteriorate. Regular monitoring will give you the opportunity to modify and alter your plan, if needed. There is nothing wrong with modifying your plan so dramatically that it is a radical departure from your initial plan. The key to a successful change plan is its adaptability. Change projects should be revised and updated on a regular basis to ensure success.

ASSESS YOUR CHANGE-MANAGEMENT SKILLS

Evaluate how well you handle and manage change by answering the following statements according to the scoring options.

1 Never
2 Occasionally
3 Frequently
4 Always

1. I have an open-minded perspective about change. ____

2. I make sure my own behaviour is flexible and adaptable. ____

3. I find opportunities to be different and seek creative ways in my approach to change. ____

4. I involve everyone who should be involved. ____

5. I listen to ideas for change from my team members. ____

6. I react positively to the demands for change. ____

7. I find ways to keep up with market demands. ____

8. I ensure that my team members have the necessary training and preparation to handle the change. ____

9. I have communicated the reasons for the change. ____

10. I don't assume my team members know everything.
    I ask them. ____

11. I make sure everyone knows the benefits to them. ____

12. I ask for my team members' input and feedback regularly. ____

13. I am careful not to create false impressions about the
    impact of change. ____

14. I regularly hold meetings to review plans. ____

15. I have a system in place for handling resistance. ____

16. I take all resistance seriously and deal with it appropriately. ____

17. I have effective contingency plans available to modify the plan. ____

18. I ensure that revised objectives are communicated clearly
    to everyone. ____

19. I keep setting targets to continuously move change forward. ____

20. I recognise, reward and celebrate successful change. ____

Total ____

Interpret Your Score

Add up your total score and check your level of skill. There is always room for improvement. Identify what areas you feel you need to work on and make a plan to hone your skills.

1–26 You have a tendency to resist change or don't see the benefits that change brings. Learn to overcome your fears and determine what your reasons are for resisting change.

27–52 You have a good understanding of the need for change. The more you develop your skills, the more proficient you will be.

53–80 You are a change agent with necessary understanding and knowledge to create and manage change. Remember that change is a constant and that it is a never-ending process requiring continuity.

Building a creative organisation has four steps.

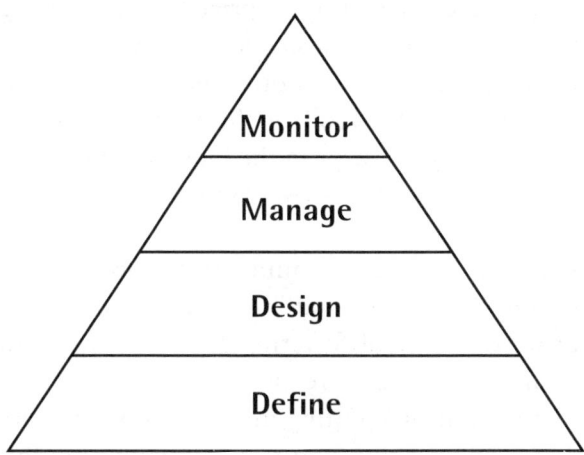

1. **Define the culture.**
   When changing a culture, you must first determine how your company will define creativity and innovation. If you don't spend adequate time on this first step, you'll have enormous difficulties throughout the rest of the process.
2. **Design a process.**
   Ideas are useless unless they can be put into motion. Making sure that ideas can eventually be translated into a tangible bottom-line result is key to devising a process that supports the culture. Prioritising and implementing ideas are very hard to do. Ideas can be implemented in one of two ways: effectively or ineffectively. The process must allow an idea to flow from conception to implementation without

wasting the resources of time, money and employee motivation. The process should include evaluation, checkpoints and specific outcomes to ensure that the idea becomes a reality.

For various reasons, not all ideas can be immediately implemented. There are three steps required to ensure that all ideas are evaluated appropriately. First, sifting has to take place to determine which ideas are workable. How will they create meaningful improvement? Second, you must devise a plan to track all of the ideas. Third, your team members have to be kept in the loop of communication so that they know what they contribute is important. How will you do this?

3. **Manage the creative and innovative process.**
   Managing the creative and innovative process is critical to ensuring success and fostering an environment that supports and encourages creativity. There can be no double standards. It means putting into place standards and practices that support this culture and making sure that everyone within the organisation follows them on a daily basis. It also means that any new hires are informed and understand that creativity and innovation are essential to the growth and future success of your business (and that creativity and innovation are expected of them).

4. **Monitor for continuous improvement.**
   Nothing describes continuous improvement better than the Japanese strategy of 'kaizen'. The word 'kaizen' means gradual, unending improvement; doing 'little things' better; setting and achieving ever-higher standards. 'Kaizen' is a customer-driven strategy for improvement. Companies that use 'kaizen' don't let a day go by without making meaningful improvements.

'One per cent improvement in 1,000 things is better than 1,000 per cent improvement in one thing.'
Tom Peters

An organisation that places emphasis on the philosophy of continuous improvement will ensure that more creative ideas can be implemented. The sooner companies use this approach, the better off they will be. When your team members use this continuous-improvement approach, they will find ways to make low-cost or no-cost improvements that will have a positive impact on the financial results. This is exciting!

Conlan Management Consultants practised this four-step method very successfully by getting its employees to gather ideas from the company's projects as well as day-to-day business activities. One of the assignments given to the new hires was to investigate the customers' perception of the delivery of service. The feedback uncovered some major discrepancies, which might otherwise have been continued indefinitely.

A large manufacturing plant was experiencing problems after a major restructuring had taken place. Employees were given the task of finding ways to resolve the situation. Corrections were made and the percentage of errors in manufacturing was drastically reduced.

It's important to be able to determine the effectiveness of the new ideas you have implemented. Today, there are many software programs you can use to create tracking reports.

In a weekly meeting that takes no longer than half an hour, managers scan a spreadsheet that determines how much time employees allocated to various tasks and projects. Managers then determine what resources are being used and whether too much time is being spent on a new idea or in a particular area. They are then able to make the appropriate changes.

Taking the time to establish the components that fall into these four steps ensures that creativity and innovation continue.

Long after the death of Walt Disney, his corporation continues to thrive on the basis of what he created more than 70 years ago. Every time an idea from an employee is implemented, the traits and qualities essential for sustaining a culture of creativity and innovation are reinforced.

NEGATIVE ATTITUDES DESTROY CREATIVITY

Albert Einstein once said, 'Great spirits have always encountered violent opposition from mediocre minds.' Nothing destroys creativity faster than the negative attitudes of others. In 1899, Charles H Duell, commissioner of the US Office of Patents, was known to have stated in a report to President McKinley, 'Everything that can be invented has been invented'. He even went so far as to argue that the patent office should be abolished.

Many years ago, the president of the Michigan Savings Bank advised Henry Ford's attorney that it wouldn't be wise to invest in the Ford Motor Company: 'The horse is here to stay, but the automobile is only a novelty – a fad.'

Or how about this voice of negativity: 'Video won't be able to hold on to any market it captures after the first six months. People will soon get tired of staring at a plywood box every night.' This was expressed by Daryl F Zanuck, the head of 20th Century Fox movie studio, commenting on television in 1946.

Negative people prefer to remain in their comfort zones. They jam their creative imaginations with self-defeating beliefs and negativity. This very often results in complete inaction and very little motivation. This behaviour is contagious, and, consequently, negativity sometimes derails people who have creative abilities. Keep in mind that while you're struggling with

'Who the hell wants to hear actors talk?'
Harry M. Warner, president, Warner Brothers Pictures, 1927

your fears and doubts about whether or not something can be done, somebody else is out there doing it.

Negativity is more evident today than ever before. Negativity is seen as realistic, and being positive is considered unrealistic. We are encouraged to look for negatives before positives. For example: The realist, not the visionary, will receive trust; the optimist, not the pragmatist, will be considered to have something wrong with her (i.e., 'Why is she so happy?').

The average workplace is often plagued by this invisible epidemic of negativity. It is a destructive force that invades and takes hold with or without harmful intent. Your attitude sets the tone for your team members, either positively or negatively. Your attitude counts! Finding ways to overcome negativity is essential for both your and your team members' performance on the job.

Before Ella Fitzgerald became a famous singer, her lifelong dream was to become a doctor. Then one night, she participated in an amateur talent contest at Harlem's Apollo Theater. Once she was on stage, she froze. The audience broke out in laughter! The laughter was soon replaced by awe when she sang songs that her mother had once sung to her. She was able to silence the audience with her incredible talent and won $25. From that moment on, she embarked on a singing career and became a legend in entertainment. She overcame her fear by maintaining a positive attitude.

Everybody has the ability to be creative, but attitude often interferes with that ability. Knowing that attitude is a major factor in creativity makes a difference in how you deal with behaviours of your team members. Set a goal to create an environment in which your team members will be able to develop their skills.

> 'When it comes to critics, remember that nobody will ever get ahead of you as long as they are kicking you in the seat of the pants.'
> Tony Randall

CREATIVITY KILLERS

Building an innovative organisation means eliminating creativity killers, which can become rampant and have an adverse effect in the workplace.

Routines and Regimentation

Routines, habits, ruts! They're all brain deadening! They are also the enemies of creativity. Without the challenge of doing things differently, employees are likely to do the same things in the same way day after day.

Routines keep your team members in their comfort zones. This is exactly where you don't want them to be. If an organisation's systems, processes, technology and leadership remain static, team members aren't expected to do anything differently. Habits turn into routines and routines become ruts. As a result, creativity is stifled, negativity becomes rife, and productivity and profits decrease.

Many of us have succumbed to routines, conformity and traditions. Change this by doing something differently every day so that you become comfortable with change and adaptable to changing circumstances.

An organisation's customer service had declined quite considerably because departments were not cooperating with one another. This was having an adverse effect on customers. One reason for this decline: employees were not enjoying their work. The challenge was to find a way to make their jobs more fun, exciting and challenging, which ultimately would improve their customers' experiences. The solution was cross-training. People switched jobs. Initially there was a period of scepticism, but this did not last long and the results were outstanding. Changing jobs gave employees a whole new perspective on how important all their efforts were. Individuals now experienced

'A new idea is delicate. It can be killed by a sneer or a yawn; it can be stabbed to death by a quip and worried to death by a frown.'
Charles Brower

'We have been taught to believe that negative equals realistic and positive equals unrealistic.'
Susan Jeffers

variety in their day-to-day jobs, and the customer service feedback improved beyond all expectations.

When we become too comfortable with the way things are, we are unlikely to make changes. This is when we become complacent. Consider being more flexible. Learn to be spontaneous by being willing to do things differently. Practise doing something different every day. Get into the habit of doing something on the spur of the moment. Drive a different route to work. Change your daily routines. Introduce different activities into your meetings. Experience something new as often as possible. Breaking habits and changing routines will open up many opportunities.

Habits, routines and ruts that are ineffective don't have a place. With business in a perpetual state of flux, you can't allow your team or yourself to become accustomed to repeating the same old behaviours day after day.

List three things you can do differently:

1. _____

   _____

2. _____

   _____

3. _____

   _____

Fear

Fear can strip you of your most valuable resources: creativity, mental dexterity, the ability to make decisions. Fear and self-doubt cause paralysis and kill off creative thinking. When fear invades an organisation, employees begin to react instead of respond. Fear limits innovative and imaginative thinking and can cause negativity. It can be totally immobilising.

Fear comes in many forms. Consider the following four most prevalent reasons for fear.

1. Fear of making mistakes

> 'Life is not to be feared but to be understood.'
> Marie Curie

Not allowing your employees to make mistakes is by far the deadliest killer of productivity and idea generation in an organisation. When people are afraid to make mistakes, they will not take risks. Avoiding mistakes is avoiding progress. There is very little opportunity for improvement when people become reluctant to take risks.

Mistakes are essential to growing ideas. Mistakes aren't done on purpose, but breakthrough ideas and solutions can't always be found without them. Creative people will push the boundaries when trying for something new. They will make more mistakes than those who are less imaginative. Bill Gates makes a point of hiring people who have previously made mistakes because this shows that they take risks.

Many inventions have resulted from mistakes.

Artificial dye was discovered by William Perkins, a British chemist, while trying to create a synthetic quinine. When the experiment failed, he noticed that there was a purple stain left behind. Instead of creating quinine, he created the beginning of the synthetic dye industry – by mistake.

> 'A person who never made a mistake never tried anything new.'
> Albert Einstein

Alexander Graham Bell invented the telephone by mistake. He was attempting to invent a hearing device and invented the telephone instead.

Roberto Goizueta, who was CEO of Coca-Cola, is known for his lasting contribution, which was a mistake – the introduction of New Coke in 1985. Realising his mis-

112

take, he had the courage to reverse that decision by reintroducing 'Classic' Coke.

Even experts make mistakes. Haloid, a small research firm founded in 1906, offered the sales rights of its '914' paper copier to IBM in the late 1950s. Not sure what to do, IBM hired Arthur D Little, a big consulting firm, to analyse the product's potential. Three months later, Arthur D Little recommended against the acquisition on the basis that the worldwide potential for these copier machines was less than 5,000 units. In just 10 years, Haloid was generating over $1 billion annually. Haloid is now known as Xerox!

There will be no risk taking where the fear of making mistakes is prevalent. You can't separate creativity from risk taking. The two go hand in hand. If you want your team members to be more creative, then you will need to eliminate the fear of making mistakes. People may be afraid of looking incompetent, looking like fools or even losing their jobs. The antidote must be an environment that is easy going and comfortable, enough so that people feel relaxed and confident.

Your approach to handling mistakes can be either constructive or destructive. An effective leader or manager might say, 'You made a mistake. How might you do it differently?' This gives employees an opportunity to find a solution and to think creatively. Your team members will be more willing to experiment with ideas if they are not penalised for making a mistake. If you punish them, you will achieve exactly the opposite of what you want to achieve.

It is rumoured that an IBM executive made a $1 million mistake. He went to Tom Watson, who was chairman of the board of IBM at the time, and said, 'I suppose you want my

> 'If you want to succeed, double your failure rate.'
> Tom Watson, former IBM Chairman

resignation.' Tom Watson replied, 'We just invested a million dollars in your education. You aren't going anywhere!'

⚡ **List three things you can do differently:**

1. _____

_____

2. _____

_____

3. _____

_____

---

2. **Fear of looking foolish**

Many people will not speak up due to the fear of being ridiculed. Their fear of being humiliated discourages them from expressing who they are, and expressing opinions and points of view.

It's important to build an environment where your team members feel safe enough to be able to voice their points of view. The following example of what not to do makes a valid point.

An organisation's sales had reached an all-time low. When a young sales executive offered a suggestion, her sales manager blurted out, 'That's the dumbest idea I've heard in a long time. If you were a man, I'd kick your ass!'

It's bad enough when a fellow team member passes judgement. When the leader does it, it's a mortal sin. When there are no rules in place for courtesy or conduct in meetings, people will not speak up!

> **List three things you can do differently:**
>
> 1. _____
>   _____
> 2. _____
>   _____
> 3. _____
>   _____

3. Fear of rejection

The majority of people have a desire to be liked. To risk being liked is to risk being rejected. You must have a good sense of yourself as well as high self-esteem to avail yourself of other people's value judgements. Ironically, the older we become, the stronger the fear of rejection. Jack Canfield, author of *How to Build High Self-Esteem*, says, 'As children, we were encouraged more than we are as adults.'

As a leader, it is your responsibility to provide an environment where the risk of rejection is non-existent.

> **List three things you can do differently:**
>
> 1. _____
>   _____
> 2. _____
>   _____
> 3. _____
>   _____

4. Fear of the unknown

Fear of the unknown keeps us in our comfort zone (CZ). Anytime we are out of our comfort zone, we are challenged at both the physical and psychological levels. We all have our own behavioural comfort zone. There is a part of us that desires change and is willing to move to the edge of the zone, and there is a part of us that wants to remain in the middle of the zone where we are isolated from any change. The reality is that the closer we stay to the middle, the harder it is to adapt to change.

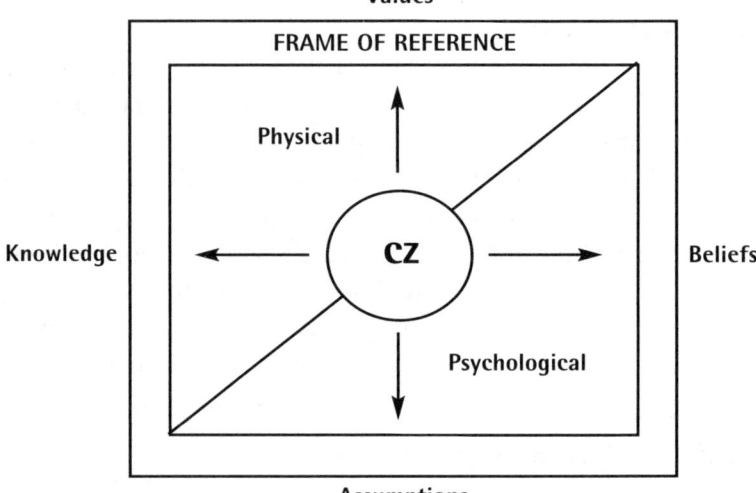

This can be one of the biggest reasons for your employees being uncreative and resistant. You will need to develop and implement a strategy to overcome it. It is imperative to make stepping out of the comfort zone a non-threatening experience. Do this by:

- Training to develop their skills.
- Keeping them informed.
- Showing how the change relates to them.
- Asking for their input.

List three ways you can assist your team with stepping outside the comfort zone:

1. _____

   _____

2. _____

   _____

3. _____

   _____

Criticism and Judgement

Oh, the voice of judgement! Imagine for just a minute that the Kellogg brothers, who had inadvertently created a cold cereal in the late 1800s, had listened to the criticism they received. They were condemned by marketing experts who predicted failure by saying the new product was horse food! The name for this cold cereal is still known today. We call it Corn Flakes!

'All things are difficult before they are easy.'
Unknown

Had Alexander Graham Bell listened to the voice of judgement from his banker, the telephone might never have been in our lives. His banker told him, 'Get out of my bank with that ridiculous toy!' That ridiculous toy was one of the first telephones Bell ever made.

The Post-it Note invention was almost killed by the voice of judgement. In 1974, Art Fry, an employee at 3M, invented these 'sticky notes'. He got tired of the loss of tiny bits of paper marking musical verses in his hymn book. One day, he made some papers with adhesive backing. These worked so well that 3M presented the idea to office-supply distributors who thought they were silly. Yet 3M persisted and did not allow the voices of judgement to deter them. The little pads were mailed to secretaries of large companies. The idea stuck. Introduced in 1980, these Post-it Notes bring in well over $400 million in annual revenue. The voice of judgement can kill an idea in a second: 'It'll never work. That's about the dumbest idea I ever heard. It'll cost too much.' Critical comments are all too common.

In order to foster creativity and imaginative thinking, we must create a safe environment in which people can express their thoughts and feelings without judgement and fear of criticism. Often the expressed judgement of a boss, co-worker or instructor will kill an idea that has some potential.

Feedback is often not offered when things are going well, yet the minute team members do something wrong, criticism is quickly delivered.

You never know who might have that one idea or formula that will take your company to an unequivocal position. Criticism of an idea or suggestion cuts off the valuable flow of creativity and enthusiasm. It's almost like saying the person's idea is stupid and should be discounted. The next time this person has an idea, she will keep it to herself. But this new idea might have been the one you needed to hear.

Further, when employees feel discounted and unimportant, they begin to treat other people (including customers), systems and equipment the same way. This ultimately sabotages your success and destroys huge potential.

When it comes to creating an environment that will stimulate the imagination of your people, you must find ways to rid your organisation of the fear of criticism, which squelches ideas and kills optimism.

> **List three ways you can create a less critical environment:**
>
> 1. _____
>   _____
> 2. _____
>   _____
> 3. _____
>   _____

Micromanagement

Very often there is a tendency to micromanage. Micromanagement is 'overcontrol', which impedes your team members' potential. This is counterproductive. It leads to demoralised and unwilling employees. A leader who overcontrols actually practises rigidity in thinking! This is definitely not conducive to creative thinking. Some people in leadership positions think that the position they hold gives them absolute authority, so they push to the extent that they micromanage. Effective leaders know that they do not achieve production through constraint, control and limitation, but by providing opportunities.

In reality, micromanagement stifles creativity! It causes people to be afraid to make mistakes. It makes them unwilling to take risks or to use their intuition to make decisions. They will choose to stay in their comfort zone where they feel safe. Very often the practice of micromanagement does not allow people to utilise their strengths, and it forces them to perform far below their capacity. A better approach is to develop their strengths and mould their raw talent to accomplish your desired objectives.

Making certain that everyone follows the rules and stays

> 'Heavier-than-air flying machines are impossible.'
> Lord Kelvin

> 'Our emphasis has always been to make something out of nothing rather than why you can't do something.'
> Masaru Ibuka, founder of Sony

119

'To live a creative life, we must lose our fear of being wrong.'
Joseph Chilton Pearce

within the confines of doing things 'your way' limits initiative and creativity. Control will keep things on track, but is it the best way? Today's leaders realise and understand that people drive business. Therefore, nurturing relationships rather than policing activities achieves maximum benefits. The cop mentality belongs to yesterday. It has no place in today's environment where employees need to feel valued, motivated and excited about change.

List three things you can do differently:

1. _____

_____

2. _____

_____

3. _____

_____

Complacency

When things are going well, there is often the mistaken belief that things should be left as they are. Innovative organisations, however, must remain alert to what their competitors are doing and for possible threats in the marketplace. Neglecting to do this would be comparable to playing Russian roulette! Leadership guru Peter Drucker so aptly says, 'No currently working business theory will be valid 10 years hence.'

You can lead a horse to the water, but you can't manage how it drinks.

For many years, Sears was the leader of the mail-order catalogue business. Today, the vast number of catalogues you receive does not include Sears. They became too complacent and refused to acknowledge that their competitors were a threat. These competitors were doing new and innovative things with emphasis on making the buying process easier and faster. Sears' competitors had toll-free numbers and door-to-door deliveries. Sears didn't even have an 800 number! If you placed an order, it meant you had to go down to the warehouse to pick it up!

Not embracing the future and being left behind can happen to your organisation. While you are clinging to the way things are, someone, somewhere out there, is developing a new product or service that will be the next winning formula.

We must be careful not to become complacent. There can never be a time when we say, 'I've finally reached the ultimate. Nothing can move me from this position.' Or 'I'm making the money I've always known I deserved. Now I can take it easy.' NO. It doesn't happen that way. It's easy to become complacent when times are good and we don't feel we need a lot of new ideas. However, if we want the good times to continue, it is vital to maintain flexibility and adaptability in our thinking skills.

The famous golfer Tiger Woods was not satisfied with the precision of his game. His concerns were distance and control of his short-iron shots. He wanted to change his swing. He knew that his competition was great and there was no room for complacency. He hired a golf coach to help him improve his game. He went through a 14-month period before it all 'clicked' (according to Tiger Woods). Within 60 to 90 days, he physically understood the new golf swing and could easily execute it. However, it was another 10 to 12 months before he was able to make the shift at the psychological level. The mental part of making the change was the most difficult. Tiger Woods knew he couldn't afford to be complacent.

It is important for us to realise that anytime we make a change, there is a tendency for our behaviour to revert back to the way it used to be until the new behaviour is fully ingrained.

Many leaders practise complacency without even realising

'So much of what we call "management" consists in making it difficult for people to work.'
Peter Drucker

121

it. They have a mistaken belief that their employees will naturally generate ideas. It is a rare leader who consistently devotes time and effort to ensure that ideas are constantly flowing. You get results by the way you lead. Encourage and support your team's actions on an ongoing basis.

List three things you can do differently:

1. _____

2. _____

3. _____

Rules and Regulations

'There is no point at which you can say, "Well, I'm successful now. I might as well take a nap."'
Carrie Fisher

In a world that is becoming increasingly unpredictable, rules and regulations have a tendency to keep things predictable. Yet some rules and regulations are obsolete. When rules don't serve a purpose, they hinder the generation of new ideas and initiative. Once rules get into place, however, they're very difficult to get rid of. Ever wonder why your team members don't always utilise their thinking abilities? All too often, it's because rules, regulations and constraints limit their potential. Many rules are outdated and serve little purpose except to keep procedures in place. This is not conducive to thinking differently.

There is an increase in authoritarianism when there are extreme formal structures. This does not allow people to 'take risks'. If you are to have a culture that is creative, you will need to give team members freedom from harmful bureaucratic constraints.

122

This is not to say that rules and regulations don't apply. Of course, they do! There has to be a fair amount of control and formal structure, especially when the organisation is large. Procedures, processes and controls are important for the work to get done. They also give direction to the team when they are appropriate to the task. Discarding outmoded rules will help to gain a brand new perspective. But a system of rules and regulations that drives an organisation towards routinisation and repetition will not lead to creativity and innovation.

List three things you can do differently:

1. _____
   _____
2. _____
   _____
3. _____
   _____

Poor Communication

Numerous communication studies indicate that 70 per cent of our communication is misunderstood, misconstrued or misinterpreted! Poor communication is one of the most prevalent problems in organisations and relationships.

You've probably heard these statements over and over:

'They never listen …'

'I told her how to do it …'

'That's not what I said …'

'That's not what I meant to say …'

'Why didn't you tell me that in the first place … ?'

'You don't understand …'

'If you play by the rules, there's no chance your name will enter the list with Stanley Marcus, Richard Branson and Donna Karan.' Retail industry executive, at Americas-Mart

'Why didn't you ask ... ?'
'You didn't tell me ...'

It is in the 'understanding' part of the communication process where many problems develop. In organisations, there are three main channels of communication: downward communication, upward communication and horizontal communication.

'Conformity is the jailer of freedom and the enemy of growth.'
John F. Kennedy

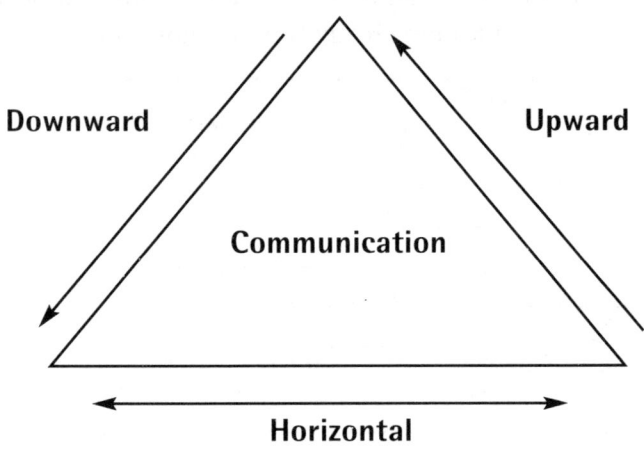

'There ain't no rules around here! We're trying to accomplish something.'
Thomas Edison

Downward communication is where misunderstandings are especially problematic. Each time the information is passed from level to level, there are parts of it that will be distorted or left out. Research has shown that only 20 per cent of the communication is clearly understood by the receiver.

Upward communication is infrequently practised and is underutilised! This is when an employee is given the opportunity to openly communicate with management. Knowing that she will be listened to, heard and her ideas considered, she will bring suggestions and ideas forward.

Horizontal communication builds better rapport and

understanding between people who are at the same level in an organisation. It includes social conversations as well as many other interpersonal communications that occur between the sender and the receiver at the point of connection. It is most effective in establishing a more cooperative environment.

You have many and varied responsibilities and duties that require your talent, competency, skill and knowledge, yet it is the skill of communicating effectively that will enable you to deal with people and handle difficult situations successfully. If all three channels are used correctly, there is no doubt you will be able to improve your communication. When there is free and open communication, there will be creativity.

The definition of success, according to Henry Ford, is, 'The ability to listen to the other person's point of view and see things from his angle as well as your own.'

List three things you can do differently:

1. _____

_____

2. _____

_____

3. _____

_____

When you have routine, fear, criticism, micromanagement, complacency, rules, regulations and poor communication, you will consistently hear your team members say, 'It won't work,' 'I don't see the point,' 'We tried it that way before,' 'Let's wait and see,' 'It can't be done.'

If what you want to hear your team members say is, 'That's

a great idea,' 'I can make it work,' 'I'll give it a try,' then use the methods that we have discussed in this chapter to involve and prepare your team for the changes that are coming. In addition, use one new mind workout every week until change is readily accepted and fully integrated within your organisation.

You have so much to gain by developing the creativity in your organisation.

CREATIVITY ENERGISES THE WORKPLACE

The benefits of creativity include the following:
- Higher profits
- Sense of ownership and pride
- Futuristic thinking
- Improved teamwork
- Effective decisions
- Less negativity
- Ability to remain flexible
- Better solutions to problems
- Trust
- Creation of new products
- Belief in company vision and leadership
- Reduced stress
- Lower levels of absenteeism
- Retention of employees

When there is an environment that supports creativity, there will be improved productivity and performance in the workplace.

Examples of Creative Organisations
Apple Computer created a user-friendly approach to personal computers. The main selling point was, 'If you can point, you

can use this computer'. This resulted in millions of dollars in sales.

The Body Shop stands out from the crowd in the retail industry. The shops have been intentionally designed to stimulate all of the senses of the customers. Everything is designed to be more memorable, including the packaging!

Chrysler's Lee Iacocca was a design fanatic. Though quality was not always up to standard, Chrysler products' unique designs put the company in an outstanding market position.

General Motors trained employees in creative problem solving at one of its forge plants. Employees discovered a $1.50 solution to prevent ring gears from sticking and breaking dies, saving the plant as much as $40,000 weekly.

Rubbermaid CEO Wolf Schmitt intentionally and systematically involved all 13,861 employees in developing new products and improving existing products. Through this approach, he was able to appeal to the mass market.

UPS, founded by Jim Casey in 1907, revolutionised the mailing business. UPS boasts access to 4 billion of the earth's 6 billion residents. It is no wonder that the company's distinctive trucks symbolise one of the world's most recognisable brands. Its tracking system is innovative and accurate, and it is because of this that many smart companies have copied their system.

Walt Disney Theme Parks have made creativity and innovation the cornerstone of their culture. In 1928, Walt and Roy Disney turned the entertainment industry upside down when they broke with tradition by introducing the first animated short feature with synchronised sound, 'Steamboat Willie'! More than seven decades later, creativity and innovation are firmly rooted in the corporate philosophy and have brought about one of the most successful corporations in the world.

> 'What?
> There's no
> door here?
> I'll build one.'
> K. Callan

Examples of Creative People

The quick-freeze process was invented by **Clarence Birdseye**, a fur trader in Labrador in the years before World War I. He emulated the Eskimos' preservation methods of quickly freezing fish and made quick-frozen foods available to the general public.

A failed idea played a key role in **Albert Einstein's** discovery of relativity. In 1887, A A Michelson and E W Morley formulated a brilliant experiment to measure the speed of light. Something went wrong and their experiment was a dismal failure. It could not detect any change in the speed of light. They dropped the experiment without knowing that they had uncovered the big clue – light always goes the same speed. It was this experiment that allowed Einstein to discover the theory of relativity years later. Not bad for a kid who was once described by a teacher as being 'mentally slow'.

'Americans like crispy cookies, not soft and chewy cookies!' Despite the adverse criticism suggesting that opening a cookie store would be a bad idea, **Debbi Fields**, the founder of Mrs Fields, went on to open her cookie store. The rest is history!

In 1937, Sylvan Goldman made his mark in history by changing the way people shop for groceries. He designed a shopping cart, which replaced shopping baskets. Shoppers increased the number of things they bought.

Charles Goodyear was obsessed with making rubber a viable product. He knew little about chemistry or chemical manufacturing, and he didn't know much about money or running a business. Even though his family had to live in a derelict rubber factory, he never let up. He had numerous failures, but he stayed focused and committed until he stumbled upon the vulcanising process.

Robert Green, a Philadelphia soda fountain operator,

invented the sundae in 1874 at a time when clergymen ruled against the act of 'sucking soda' on Sundays. Green was able to find a way around the ban by serving ice cream with sweet syrup but no soda water. The sundae was created!

At a time when he was facing financial ruin, **J C Hall** helped reinvent the American greetings-card business. He was in the business of importing elegantly engraved cards from Europe. After an entire inventory of cards was destroyed in a fire a few weeks before Valentine's Day, he had no time to reorder more cards from Europe. Hall bought a small engraving company and began producing simple designs. From that day on, he started producing more casual cards for other occasions to keep his presses running. He changed his industry!

In 1837, Englishman **Rowland Hill** proposed uniform postage regardless of the distance, lower fees and prepayment by buying and applying a stamp. Up until that revolutionary idea, mail had always been paid for by the addressee, with the fee calculated according to distance and weight. This made mailing expensive and slow. Rowland Hill eliminated what was not necessary, and the volume of mail doubled in the first four years. It quadrupled again over the next 10! Also, the English postal service became more efficient and solvent.

During the Great Depression, most cereal companies reduced advertising and cut costs. **Will Kellogg**, CEO of Kellogg's, did the opposite. He increased the size of his cereal's package, doubled his ad budget and erected the world's largest billboard in Times Square. Surviving the Depression was not all he accomplished. He went on to flourish and thrive.

When vodka arrived in America in the 1930s, nobody wanted to drink clear alcohol. The Russian immigrant who brought it in finally gave up and sold the rights for $14,000 in 1939. **John Martin**, president of Heublein, proceeded to find a way to popularise the drink by adding other ingredients to it that would colour the drink. Today, we have the Moscow Mule, Screwdriver and Bloody Mary. As of 1988, vodka sales were in the vicinity of 38 million cases a year.

In the late 1800s, **John Pemberton** invented a chemical mixture designed to 'whiten teeth and cleanse the mouth'. It didn't do what it was supposed to do but it did make an impact. His formula was called Coca-Cola! By the 1980s, Coca-Cola sales were in excess of 250 million servings each day.

Howard Schultz revolutionised an everyday product into a customer craze. Schultz elevated Starbucks, a gourmet coffee company, into a rapidly growing business. Visiting Italy during the 1980s, Schultz decided to build a national chain of Starbucks patterned after Italian coffee bars. He adapted the coffee for American tastes by offering espresso, straight and undiluted. It is not uncommon for his customers to spend $100 a month at Starbucks coffee establishments!

Fred Smith was known to have received a 'C' grade from a Yale University management professor on a paper he had written on a proposal to provide an overnight delivery service. Ironically enough, Fred Smith went on to begin Federal Express!

In an effort to keep his job as a janitor, **James Spangler** invented what was to become Hoover vacuum cleaners. He was too old to lift heavy carpet cleaning machines and he couldn't afford to quit his job. He had to find another way to clean carpets. He did!

Frank Woolworth was a struggling 21-year-old clerk in Watertown, NY, who got a great idea from his boss one day when all the unwanted inventory was placed on a five-cent table. He went on his own and started the 'Great Five-Cent Store' in Utica. It was a dismal failure. Undeterred, Frank

Woolworth opened his second store to coincide with the circus coming to town. A third of the merchandise was sold and he never looked back.

Many of these successful people suffered setbacks at one time or another. Despite their initial failures, they succeeded. The greater the risk, the greater the loss. Yet, greater risks also led to bigger payoffs.

History books are filled with stories about incredible individuals who achieved remarkable feats and inventions that made significant improvements and changes in the world. These remarkable people dared to be different and were not concerned about going against the status quo.

Quick question: Are you going to be one of those incredible people that we read about in the years to come?

CHAPTER SEVEN

BOTTOM LINE

'I don't give a damn for any man who can spell a word only one way.'
Mark Twain

Ideas are critical to the success and continued existence of any organisation, but some people do not use their creative-thinking abilities as easily as others. Effective leaders will need to make sure that they provide the resources and tools to enable all team members to become creative.

Your course of action should be to continually find new ways of doing things by using any of the mind workouts to crank up your team's thinking. When team members practise mind workouts and begin to utilise their thinking abilities with more effectiveness, they will find ways to do things better, faster, less costly and more efficiently.

To ensure that creativity thrives in your organisation, encourage team members to be consistently on the lookout for alternative ways of doing things. This is a business imperative, even when things are currently working well. Team members who continually practise thinking creatively will respond more effectively when things go wrong.

'Innovation ... endows resources with a new capacity to create wealth.'
Peter Drucker

STAY ONE STEP AHEAD

Too often we get locked into one way of doing things. So, the team's attitude is, 'If things are working, why change them?' or 'If it ain't broke, why fix it?' When the methods you use to find new ways of doing things are routine and unchanging, your team members get bored and switch off. Remember, the world is relentlessly changing, and we can never be complacent. Making improvements to routines, systems and working procedures is necessary on an ongoing basis.

THERE IS MORE THAN ONE RIGHT ANSWER

Ignite the Spark: 52 Creative Ways to Boost Productivity will equip you with effective methods to shape strategies and find alternative solutions. When you look for more than one right answer, you allow your imagination to flow. When you stop looking, you limit your choices.

> 'In differentiation, not in uniformity, lies the path of progress.'
> Louis D. Brandeis

Team members will often stop searching when they find one answer, and it can be the second or third option that is exactly what you need to solve a problem. One technique for finding alternative answers is to 'pluralise' your questions. Don't ask, 'What is the answer or solution?' Ask, 'What are the answers or the solutions?' Don't ask, 'What is the result?' Ask, 'What results are there?'

The bottom line is that you need to generate lots of ideas, solutions, answers and results to become an innovative and creative company. While you may not always be able to use all the ideas that you generate, you can be sure your team members will produce many ideas that are worthwhile. Photographers take many shots to get that one picture they are aiming for. Use this same approach for thinking, generating ideas and finding solutions. Then you will find many great ideas and ensure your company's success.

Once there were two men whose opinions differed. An

argument ensued. They decided to settle the matter by going to a judge. First, the plaintiff made his case very eloquently and persuasively. When he had finished, the judge nodded his head, saying 'That's right, that's right.'

Hearing this, the defendant jumped in and said, 'It's my turn. You haven't heard my side of the story.' The defendant made his case, also very eloquently and persuasively. When he had finished, the judge nodded his head, saying 'That's right, that's right.'

Moral of the story: Truth is all around you, and what matters is that you realise there is more than one right answer.

MIND WORKOUTS BECOME A HIGH-VOLTAGE EXPERIENCE

Finding ways to force your mind or your team members' minds to generate ideas, solve problems or process information when you are under pressure is extremely difficult. When these situations arise, certain thinking processes are necessary to induce creative thinking. You will find these mind workouts to be highly focused, which will help your team members quickly break the mould of their old thinking processes. In addition, you will need to use the four-step creativity process: preparation, incubation, illumination and verification.

USE IT OR LOSE IT

'Invention breeds invention.'
Ralph Waldo Emerson

Your brain is a muscle just like any other in your body. It needs to exercise frequently. When you don't use it, its functions weaken. It will suffer a form of mental atrophy. Keeping your brain active can be compared with keeping your body physically fit and healthy. Inactivity can cause men and women to lose significant amounts of muscle and bone mass. Left unchecked, this process continues on in later years, leading to frailty. At Tufts University, research proves that strength training can turn back the clock and make our bodies more physically and metabolically youthful. Keeping your brain active and exercised is critical to enhancing the brain's capabilities, now and in later years. Mind workouts will assist in flexing, strengthening and growing your mind power.

Mind workouts assist in making the brain more agile, flexible and ready to take on any mental challenge, whether it is creativity, performance, memory or task. These skills need to be practised in order to be honed; as you use them, you will assuredly begin to make significant improvements in everything you do.

BE PERSISTENT

We've said all along that building an ongoing creative organisation isn't easy. Creative thinking involves a lot more than just having great new ideas. Now you have to do something with those ideas. You have to be willing to adopt new values, try new behaviours, implement new methods and decide if they are working for you. It takes persistence and tenacity to make consistent creative thinking a reality, but the alternative is not an option. You don't fail until you quit.

Once upon a time there were two frogs that had the misfortune to fall into a bucket of cream. The first frog could not find a footing in the white fluid and believed there was no way to escape. He accepted his fate and drowned.

The second frog was more positive and didn't like the

'Iron rusts from disuse; water loses its purity from stagnation and in cold weather becomes frozen; even so does inaction sap the vigours of the mind.'
Leonardo da Vinci

approach of the first frog. He began thrashing around and doing whatever he could to stay alive in the bucket of cream. A short while later, the frog's churning about turned the cream into butter. He was able to crawl on top and hop out.

How persistent are you? Never give up. Nothing in the world will take the place of persistence.

MAKING IT HAPPEN

Throughout this book, we have shared our views and perspectives as well as specific tools and techniques for breakthrough thinking. Some of you might be thinking, 'What do I do with all of this now?'

This new knowledge needs to be applied to your everyday living and tasks … now and for the rest of your life. Go back through your notes, self-assessments and concepts and pick one technique or mind workout to practise. Try it. Then try another. Use, experiment and refine these tools with every situation. Gradually, in your challenge to transform your team's thinking abilities, you will begin to see dramatic changes that will benefit everyone.

The key to making it happen is to take ACTION. These mind workouts will help you achieve your goals. Their purpose is to help your team members think creatively, to stimulate and inspire them and to expand their perspectives. Putting the methods into practice will stimulate thinking and assist your team members in generating ideas. As they change the way they think, team members will begin asking, 'Why do we do it this old way when we have a new and improved way?'

The statue of a prominent archer, holding a bow and arrow in his hands ready to shoot, stood on the hill near the ancient city of Troy. Legend says the arrow was pointed in the direction of a buried chest that contained immense knowledge. Inside the chest were scrolls and letters that answered the mystery of human existence.

Over the years many men tried to follow the course indicated by the arrow but without success. One year, a man with a bold mind came to examine the situation. In no time at all, he realised that all the old methods for solving the mystery were quite useless. He would need to think about the problem in a new way.

Many warned him that this was futile and discouraged him from continuing on. The young man did not falter in his quest for finding a way. Begrudgingly, his opponents began to feel a certain amount of respect for this young man.

Every day the young man patiently sat and looked at the statue, trying to discover something unusual, different or even obvious. He noticed that every afternoon at three o'clock the shadow of the arrow pointed between two distant mountain peaks. It was at the base of those two peaks that he found the treasure of knowledge he so fervently wanted. From that moment on, all those who made an earnest attempt to think in new ways about their problems found the wisdom they wanted. The young man was always remembered by the people of the ancient city of Troy with immense admiration for having dared to be different and a nonconformist.

The bottom line is that the consistent application of these mind workouts will help you and your team members achieve tremendous breakthroughs in traditional thinking. It will also help you identify new and effective approaches to problem solving, decision making and profit generation. Using these mind workouts will ultimately lead to tangible solutions that

> 'Necessity is the mother of invention.'
> Plato

fulfil needs, make a difference and give you the leading edge.

We've given you the techniques, tools and strategies. Now it's up to you. It's time to take ACTION and crank up your team's thinking!

We wish you much success!

CHAPTER EIGHT

52 MIND WORKOUTS TO BOOST PRODUCTIVITY

1. CLEARING THE MIND

What It Is
A technique to assist us in making a rapid transition from having thoughts and issues on our mind to focusing and giving full attention to a meeting's discussion, problem or challenge of the moment.

What You'll Need
- Stopwatch or timer
- Flip chart or whiteboard
- Markers

How It Works
Team members have one minute in which to briefly share whatever is on their minds.

This is not a time for discussion or problem solving. It is simply a time to share a statement of what is on each person's mind, whether it is simple venting or sharing personal news.

It's OK to pass.

If someone brings up a subject that is worthy of discussion by the group, put it on your 'Parking Lot' (a flip chart or whiteboard where subjects that should be discussed later are written or 'parked' until a later time) or note it for later discussion.

Once each person has a turn, get down to the scheduled agenda or the problem at hand.

If the group is large, the sharing can be done in small groups with members of each group sharing within their group.

2. GROUND RULES

What It Is
A set of behaviours to abide by when attending team meetings. Once the ground rules have been agreed upon, post them near the front of the room and refer to them as needed.

What You'll Need
- Flip chart
- Markers

How It Works
Members of the group propose acceptable ground rules. These rules should be discussed and agreed upon at the first meeting of the group. When the group has completed the list, ask the entire group if there are any ground rules that anyone cannot live with or support. If so, change as necessary. Be sure that you have 100 per cent buy-in to all ground rules.

During the meeting, any member can remind anyone who strays from the agreed upon ground rules.

Examples of ground rules include:

- Begin and end on time.
- Turn off cellular phones.
- Listen to other ideas without judgement.
- No side talking
- Stick to the subject.
- Stay on schedule.
- Offer solutions.
- Don't complain, make negative comments or lecture others.

3. STRUCTURED QUESTIONS

What It Is

A specific process for addressing agenda items that avoids excess discussion or going around in circles. Structured questions are necessary to gain full understanding in communication.

What You'll Need

- List of questions for each participant
- Flip chart
- Markers

How It Works

Before your meeting, decide on the purpose and desired result of your agenda items. Then, determine the best questions you need to guide your discussion of the following categories:

- **Facts:** What are the facts?
- **Feelings:** What feelings do we have about this?
- **Brainstorm:** What alternatives do we have? What ideas?
- **Pros:** What is right or good about each alternative? What would be the benefit of this alternative? What quality can we expect?

- **Cons:** What are the negatives of each alternative? What are the time parameters? What are the budget constraints? What are the personnel requirements?
- **Agreement:** What should we do? What should we not do? What do we all agree upon?
- **Next steps:** What are the next steps? Who must we communicate with? How will we measure success? How will we follow through? How will we follow up?

Let the group see all of the questions from the beginning. It will help them focus and be patient.

Ask the group to answer only one question at a time.

Record all answers.

4. BALL TOSS

What It Is

A technique used to stimulate thinking in a spontaneous and exciting way. It generates options and solutions to current challenges or problems.

What You'll Need

Ball

How It Works

During meetings, give a ball to one participant and ask her for her opinion or knowledge on the subject at hand. When this participant finishes speaking, she then tosses the ball to the next participant, who is then to speak. Continue to pass the ball until all group members have spoken.

Repeat this rotational process until all ideas have been satisfactorily discussed.

Time permitting, particpants can go more in depth to discuss possible actions.

Option
Participants sit in a circle and the ball is rolled to one participant who is asked for input. When this participant is finished speaking, she rolls the ball to the participant she selects. Continue to pass the ball until all group members have spoken.

5. VISUAL BRAINSTORMING

What It Is
A method of expressing ideas in a tangible form. Team members express their thoughts and ideas by drawing them out as they think. This method can be done individually or in a group. Don't burden this process by making judgements about the ability to draw. Just do it. The idea is to get the thoughts into a visual form.

What You'll Need
• Large sheets of paper
• Coloured markers

How It Works
Define the problem or need.

Ask the team members to draw their ideas as they think of them.

Do not make judgements.

After the visual brainstorming is complete, hold a 'report back' session where team members explain their drawings.

Have them evaluate what has been done and what conclusions they can make for solving the problem.

Option

When you do this exercise in a group, you can have one team member draw for everyone on the team, or all members may participate in drawing.

An example of this exercise is found in Chapter 4. Hal Rosenbluth used this method to get his employees to draw pictures of their work climate.

6. METAPHORICAL THINKING

What It Is

The use of metaphors helps to explain and clarify the meaning of specific issues when information is difficult to understand or to explain in simple terms. Metaphors are a good way of developing creativity. They help people learn and think in new ways.

What You'll Need
- Definition of metaphor*
- Stopwatch or timer

How It Works

Before the meeting:

Identify the point you want to emphasise or explain. Think of what is important to your team members and how they will be able to relate. Brainstorm possible analogies and metaphors and select one or two that you will use.

> *Metaphor – a representation or a figurative expression for something. The key to metaphorical thinking is comparison. A metaphor suggests comparison between things or concepts, thus helping to explain them. 'Life is a room full of open doors'.

At the meeting:
Introduce the topic.

Make sure everyone understands the definition of a metaphor.

Explain why you are asking the group to create metaphors. Explain how metaphors will be used.

Give examples of your metaphors.

Ask team members to create a metaphor for a problem you're currently dealing with.

Allow the group five minutes for thinking on the stated topic.

Ask the group what conclusions can be drawn.

Example
A company is experiencing limited sales, even though there is a high demand for similar products. A metaphor was created for the company as the first step to solve the problem. It was decided that the company was a full-service restaurant. The menu was the product line, which was large but had restrictions. The individual chefs – the division managers – realised that there was no consistency in the menu options. Consequently, this led to needing specialised waiters – salespeople. If a customer couldn't buy hamburgers from a fish waiter or pasta from a steak waiter, it was quite obvious that a large, restricted product line was confusing to the customers. This was determined to be the main reason for the limited sales!

Then discuss the following with team members:
• Does the number of similarities surprise you?
• What are the ways in which you can use this metaphor?
• What action guidelines does this point towards for us?

7. CHAIR EXCHANGE

What It Is

During meetings, participants are asked to sit in different places, next to different people. This is mentally stimulating and discourages cliques. It puts people in a position to discuss subjects with members of the team with whom they don't have usual contact and builds teamwork through new alliances.

What You'll Need

A plan for reseating

How It Works

This can be done through predetermined discussion groups where a mix of people is created based on different levels within the organisation, longevity on the job, diversity and perspective.

Simply assign numbers to the members of the group and have the group break into small working teams by number.

Another way is to put stickers on name tags or tent cards. Have people with the same style stickers move into groups together.

8. POSTERS

What It Is

A visual brainstorming technique to involve team members in problem solving.

What You'll Need

- Flip chart or Post-it Easel Pad
- Markers
- Post-it Notes

How It Works

Adhere posters/wall charts/flip-chart paper to the wall around the room with specific problems, issues or ideas written across the top. Give participants Post-it Notes and ask them to write their ideas on the Post-it Notes and stick the notes onto the relevant poster. Break into small groups to discuss these ideas and/or evaluate them for implementation.

Option

Adhere Post-it Easel Pad paper to a wall in an employee area with a statement of the specific problem or request for suggestions across the top. Leave the big sticky in its place for the period of time you deem to be adequate. This gives employees sufficient time to suggest their ideas, add to or build on ideas without pressure.

9. TOYS

What It Is

A way to create a playful environment to effectively stimulate team members' thinking by engaging their thinking processes.

What You'll Need

Some simple toys that won't require any mental concentration, make noise, or distract others in the group, such as the following:

- Playdough
- Tinkertoys®
- Lego™ toys
- Coloured pencils/paper

- Finger puppets
- Small stuffed animals
- Koosh® balls
- Rubik's Cube®

How It Works

Explain to meeting participants that the toys can be played with individually, at any time during the meeting and without permission. They are not to distract other team members.

At the end of the meeting, you may ask participants either to leave toys in the room or take them as souvenirs.

You may want to ask participants for reactions to having these toys available.

10. MUSIC

What It Is

Music stimulates the brain's creative centres. Choose music as a natural enhancer to aid a certain type of thinking. It is used either to calm or energise thinking processes. Music will help reconnect team members to ideas that they might have worked on previously.

What You'll Need

- Music player (CD or tape player)
- Music that will support the theme or mood you want to create.

How It Works

Play the music prior to the meeting and during breaks. Tunes from the '50s, '60s, '70s and '80s, soundtracks from movies and other upbeat melodies get people talking and in a good mood before and after a meeting.

During 'quiet time' or 'thinking time,' play relaxing music. Instrumentals allow for more creative thinking. The rhythmical flow of classical music such as Bach, Vivaldi and Pachelbel will help get people in the 'zone'.

Music with lyrics should support the planned agenda or main theme you want to reinforce.

Whether you're trying to raise energy levels or create a more relaxed environment, music can be very conducive to thinking processes.

Option
Make a 'power tape' of tunes that you can use to change moods for the appropriate thinking required.

11. 'RAP' SOLUTIONS

What It Is
A presentation of ideas that is both visual and auditory.

What You'll Need
- A selection of music with rhythm that is pleasing to the group
- Paper

How It Works
Ask group members to solve a problem or invent a new way of doing something.

Have them prepare some visual aids to explain to the group what they have done and how they have done it.

Have them present their material in 'rap' style, verbally reviewing the visualised material to synchronised music.

12. BRAIN WRITING

What It Is

Brain writing is a method of brainstorming in which participants brainstorm ideas or solutions to a situation without verbally communicating with one another.

What You'll Need

- Music
- Index cards
- Pens

How It Works

The team should sit in a circle.

Present the issue. Allow a short time for thinking.

Play some instrumental music and ask each participant to write down her comments on an index card.

Participants must have their own index cards. Ask them not to think about form, but to just write anything that they think about the issue.

Participants must simultaneously pass their card to the participant to the right of them.

The next participant now adds her ideas to the index card. If the participant has a mental block, the participant passes the card to the right and continues with the next index card and so on.

This exercise can be used when you need to brainstorm information quickly. It is especially effective when you have team members who are uncomfortable speaking in front of the group, or when you have some participants who tend to dominate conversations.

If you have enough time, ask questions such as the following:

- Can you see any value in trying some of these suggestions?
- Did the ideas from others trigger ideas or solutions for you?
- What lessons did we learn about reaching out to others for their assistance?

13. NINE-DOT EXERCISE

What It Is

The nine-dot exercise is designed to challenge assumptions. Many people make the assumption that the lines must not extend beyond the imaginary square formed by the dots, the paper must be flat, the lines must be thin, or you may not fold the paper. The trick is to challenge these assumptions.

Give your participants the Citibank example. In 1980, costs were cut by the implementation of automatic tellers. Initially, these automatic tellers were designated for use by the small depositors to the machines. The automatic tellers were unpopular, and Citibank stopped using them in 1983 on the assumption that customers preferred human tellers.

A few months later, this assumption was challenged when it was discovered that the small depositors did not like using the automatic tellers because they perceived them to be for second class customers.

Later, when there was no class distinction made, the automatic tellers became extremely successful.

What You'll Need
At least four nine-dot exercises
per participant

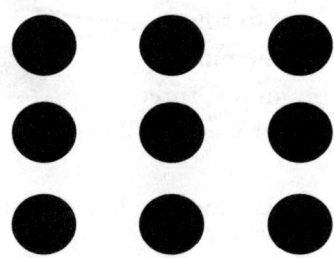

How It Works

Challenge your participants to find one to four different ways of connecting the dots.

Connect all the dots using no more than four straight lines, without lifting your pencil and without retracing your steps. Allow three minutes for participants to do this.

If anyone solves the puzzle, invite them to come forward and show the others how it is done.

If no one solves it, show the group how to do it.

This solution is commonplace and many of your team members will see it. Many will still not remember how to do it.

1. Using four lines –
   see illustration.

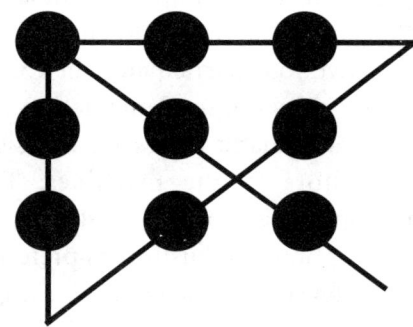

Assumption: Lines must not extend beyond the dots.

2. If you draw lines that just touch the dots, you can solve the puzzle in just three strokes as follows.

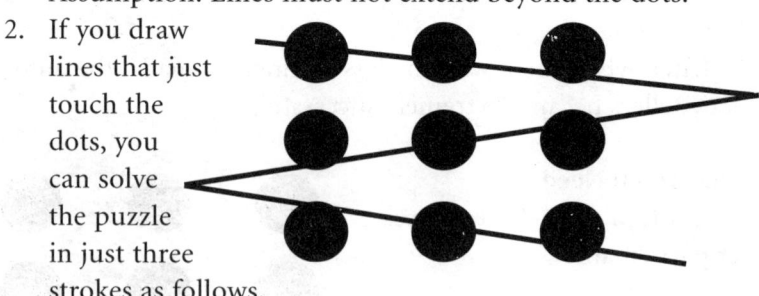

Assumption: Lines must pass through the centre of the dots.

3. Use one big fat line to connect all the dots at once.

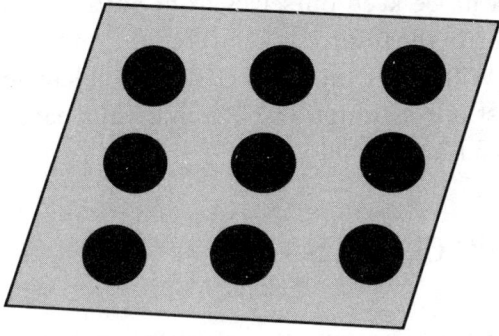

   Assumption: Lines must be thin.
4. Roll the paper into a tube. It's possible to connect the dots with a spiral.
   Roll paper – see illustration.

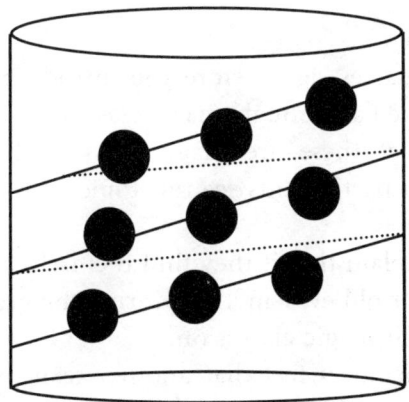

   Assumption: The paper must be flat.
   Debrief the exercise.
   Why was it so difficult?

Why do we want to be aware that we put limits on our thinking? How can we keep ourselves from putting boundaries on our thinking in the future? What were some of the assumptions we made? Will we be more effective at problem solving if we can get past our assumptions? Remind your participants that thinking is a learned skill.

14. MAGIC GLASSES

What It Is
A method used to encourage participants to look at old issues in new ways.

What You'll Need
A pair of silly looking glasses for each team member

How It Works
Pass out the glasses right before you introduce the topic that should be looked at through 'magic glasses'.

Explain that these are magic glasses which have been designed to let participants see this topic with a new perspective.

Further explain that if they find themselves looking at the topic with their old eyes anytime during the programme, they should put their magic glasses on.

If team members feel that another team member is still using an old way of looking at things, they may ask that team member to put on her magic glasses or they may offer to trade magic glasses in order to get a different perspective.

This not only aids your team members with breaking old habits and perspectives, but it also is a lot of fun!

15. BRAINSTORMING

What It Is

Brainstorming is one of the easiest strategies for finding creative solutions and new ideas. Brainstorming was developed by Alex Osborn and was designed to help people express ideas and, specifically, to suspend judgement until the end of discussion. All ideas are listed and then improved upon, combined or changed. Only then are ideas evaluated for final ruling.

What You'll Need

- Flip chart or whiteboard
- Markers

How It Works

The usual method is to introduce the topic and the purpose of the brainstorming session. It is recommended at the beginning of a meeting to either state the brainstorming rules or refer to them. A brainstorming session should be an uninhibited environment where team members feel safe to be imaginative.

Ask a team member to record all ideas (words, phrases or pictures) on a flip chart or whiteboard as they are stated.

Be sure that all participants understand that in brainstorming:

- All ideas and information are appreciated.
- Everyone in the group contributes.
- Nothing is too silly or far-out.
- There is no criticism of anyone's ideas.
- It's important to generate quantity of ideas versus quality of ideas.
- Another person's idea can be added to.
- All ideas are written down on a flip chart.
- Ideas are not analysed at this time. They are simply expressed.

Use approximately the last half of a brainstorming session for evaluating all ideas.

Option

Once everyone feels that they have exhausted all of their ideas, ask team members to come forward and place check marks next to all the ideas on the chart that they feel are worthy of further discussion. The ideas with the most check marks are discussed first; thereafter, all are discussed, one by one, and evaluated.

16. FIVE WHYS

What It Is

A technique to access information and create dialogue in order to get to the bottom of an issue or problem. This method is also very effective for challenging assumptions.

How It Works

Simply ask 'why' at least five times during the discussion about your specific problem and about each answer you receive until your group feels it has discovered the core reason for the problem.

This may involve asking people at several levels of the organisation before the problem is fully understood.

Option

Divide group members into pairs. One person will present the problem; the other will try to find out the bottom line by asking five whys, if time permits.

The feedback should be done in the original pairs.

17. RIGHT/WRONG DISCUSSION

What It Is

An open discussion in a safe environment.

How It Works

Schedule time once a week to discuss objectively what's been going right, as well as what's been going wrong. This can be done either individually or with a group of team members. This is a discussion, not a 'witch hunt'. When you lay things out on the table for discussion, you create an opportunity to learn from one another and do better the next time.

This technique is most effective when an 'early win' is created. You can achieve this by utilising any information from these discussions that leads to improvement in the workplace environment and corrects a situation or situations.

Option

Can be incorporated at a 'brown bag' lunch meeting.

18. MIND MAPPING

What It Is

Mind mapping is a form of group brainstorming originated by Tony Buzan. It is used for quickly charting ideas into logical groupings when information is given in a nonsequential manner. Mind mapping allows you to see things in perspective and to prioritise efficiently to take action. The intention of mind mapping is to use random thinking without worrying about the order or organisation of ideas captured.

What You'll Need

- Flip chart or Post-it Easel Pad
- Coloured markers

How It Works

Identify specifically what you want to brainstorm and place a key word or symbol in the centre of your mind map within a circle. Members of the group brainstorm their ideas and branch out their individual ideas, which are drawn out from the centre. Typically, more important ideas will be closer to the centre and less important ideas will stem further out. Do not apply structure to this exercise by attempting to put ideas in order.

Guidelines

Starting at the centre of the page, write a word or draw a coloured image as the central theme to your mind map. Use coloured markers to enhance memory by association.

Words should be printed for clarity.

From the central theme, branches or lines are drawn towards the boundary of the page. These are the primary ideas. Each printed word should be on a line with each line connected to other lines.

Secondary branches that relate to the primary branches are then extended from the primary ones. Each secondary line/idea must relate to the primary line/idea.

More branches are drawn off the secondary branches as the third level of ideas and so on.

Once all ideas have been captured, a final ordering in terms of importance and relevance can take place.

Mind Map of Chapter 1

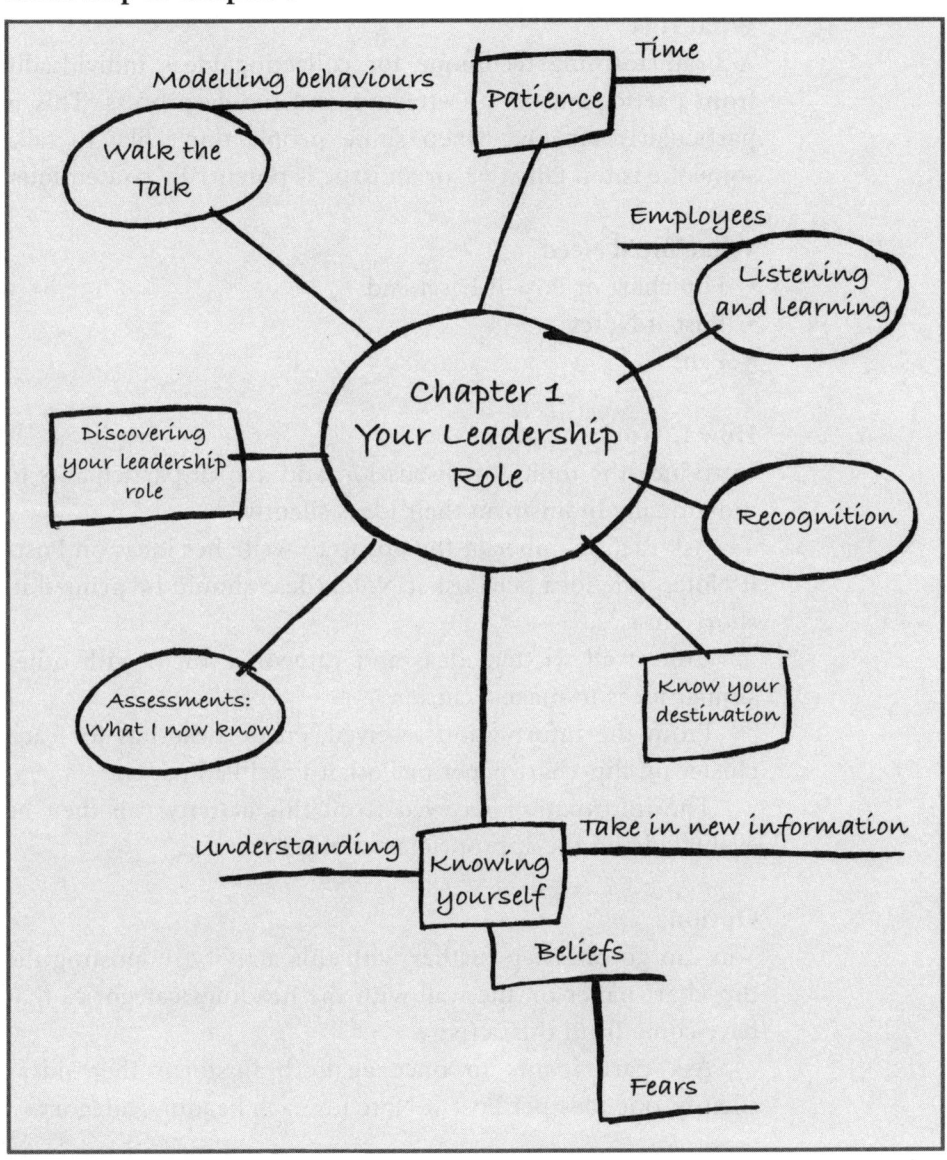

19. IDEA CLUSTERS

What It Is

A brainstorming technique for collecting ideas individually from participants in an effective and timely process. This is particularly effective when some people don't like to talk, someone is too talkative, or an issue is potentially contentious.

What You'll Need
- Flip chart or Post-it Easel Pad
- Post-it Notes
- Pens

How It Works

Introduce the topic for discussion and ask all participants to individually brainstorm their ideas silently.

Ask each member of the group to write her ideas on Post-it Notes, one idea per Post-it Note. Ideas should be printed in short phrases.

Collect all written ideas and categorise them with other similar ideas to make a cluster.

From the information received, create headings for each cluster on flip-chart paper or Post-it Easel Pad paper.

The information received from this activity can then be evaluated and the appropriate action taken.

Option

You can go one step further with this activity by posting the flip-chart paper on the wall with the headings/categories that have come from this activity.

Ask participants to once again brainstorm their ideas silently, one idea per Post-it Note for each heading/category.

When they have written their ideas, ask them to post their ideas under the appropriate heading on the large flip-chart paper.

Once you have all the ideas from your participants, the information can be evaluated for implementation.

20. CHECKLIST FOR NEW IDEAS

What It Is

A commonly used brainstorming tool to help participants think imaginatively and differently. The following is a modification of Alex Osborn's checklist. The original version can be found in Osborn's *Applied Imagination*.

How It Works

Write down the statement of the problem or the process to be changed.

Ask participants to write the different ways to change it under each set of the following questions.

PUT IT TO OTHER USES

New ways to use? Other uses if modified? What else could be made from this? Different markets?

_____

_____

_____

ADAPT

Adapt someone else's idea? Does the past offer a parallel? What can be copied? What else is like this? What other idea does this suggest?

_____

_____

_____

MODIFY

How can it be changed? Change colour, motion, sound, odour, form, shape? Change plans? Change name? What can be made better? Other packaging? Change meaning? Attitude? Marketing?

_____

_____

_____

MAGNIFY

What to add? More time? Greater frequency? Stronger? Higher? Larger? Longer? Thicker? More value? Duplicate? Multiply? Extra features? Exaggerate?

_____

_____

_____

MINIMISE

What to subtract? Condense? Make smaller? More compact? Lower? Shorter? Lighter? Omit? Streamline? Split up? Understate? What's not necessary?

_____

_____

_____

SUBSTITUTE
What else instead? Other material? Other process? Substitute people? Other colour? Other format? Other ideas? Other place?

_____

_____

_____

REARRANGE
Other layout? Other pattern? Other sequence? Interchange components? Switch cause and effect? Change pace? Change the order? Change schedule?

_____

_____

_____

REVERSE
Turn it backwards? Reverse positive and negative? Use the opposite? Turn it upside down? Reverse roles? Turn it around?

_____

_____

_____

COMBINE
Combine purposes? Combine ideas? Combine units? What materials could be combined? Combine services? Combine talents?

_____

_____

_____

Example

Sony's Walkman is an excellent example of the use of this brainstorming activity. By manipulating an existing idea into a new idea, Masaru Ibuka and his engineers created one of their best-selling electronic devices, the Walkman. They combined portable headphones with their small stereo tape recorder; minimised it by having it just play music; reversed its order by changing its function (no recorder and speakers); put it to other uses as a new notion in entertainment; substituted their market by targeting the youth; then modified their marketing campaign to target yuppies when the teenage market did not respond.

21. OPEN-ENDED QUESTIONS

What It Is

A technique for gathering information. The ability to ask the right questions is one of the most important of all creative skills. Before your meeting, determine specific open-ended questions that will elicit the type of information you need. Open-ended questions begin with the words 'who,' 'what,' 'where,' 'when,' 'which,' 'why' and 'how'.

How It Works

Open-ended questions will get you information and cannot be answered with the words 'yes' or 'no'.

At the beginning of this exercise, explain the purpose of this questioning method and what you hope to achieve.

Then ask the following questions:

- What do you think about …?
- Who should be involved …?
- What ideas do you have concerning …?

- Where can we make changes …?
- What were your reactions to …?
- Why is it that …?
- How can we do …?
- Which of these options is …?
- What (about) …?
- How can we accomplish …?
- What alternatives would you suggest …?

If you think you are getting responses that are too broad or too vague, ask another open-ended question. After you have asked all these questions, there is one more question you can ask in order to know what action will be taken.
- What's next?

22. CREATIVITY CULTURE

What It Is

A series of activities designed to get your team members to contribute ideas on a regular basis.

What You'll Need
- Web site, Intranet
- Whiteboard
- Markers

How It Works

Create a culture of creativity by letting people know that you want and value their ideas on a regular basis.
- Create a 'Good Ideas' page on your Web site and encourage everyone to contribute.
- Place a whiteboard and markers in a conspicuous place like

a break room with the subject or problem to be addressed written on the board. Advise everyone to write on the board any ideas they have pertaining to this subject.

- Document and keep good ideas in an 'Ideas File'. Then when the time is right and you implement the idea, let everyone know whose idea it was. Team members will feel good knowing their ideas were worth keeping, and they'll know you were really listening to them.
- Create an 'e-grapevine'. Use your intranet or website as a place to collect and post ideas, opinions and suggestions for improvement.
- Schedule 'agendaless' meetings. Invite people to come and just talk about whatever is on their minds. It shows that you care about them and value their opinions.

23. USING DIVERGENT AND CONVERGENT THINKING

What It Is
A six-step problem-solving technique using 'whole-brain thinking'.

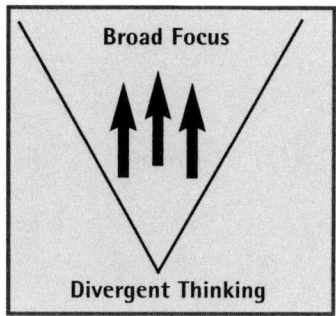

Divergence: to branch off
Divergent thinking can be compared to firing a shotgun. The focus is broad and the target is large.
- Judgement is turned off.
- Creates possibility.
- No criteria, no evaluation.

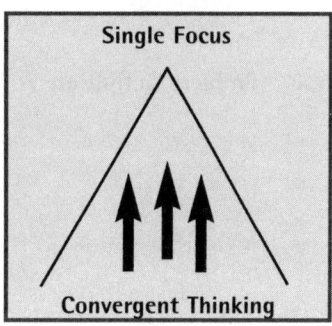

Convergence: to come together
Convergent thinking can be compared to taking aim with a pistol. The focus is narrow and pinpointed.
- Judgement is turned on.
- Creates practicality.
- Evaluated and critiqued.

How It Works
By engaging both sides of the brain in the thinking process, we are more flexible in our exploration and are likely to find more workable solutions.

		DIVERGENT	CONVERGENT
1.	Problem Finding	What problems, situations, concerns and opportunities are in this situation?	Which of these must we work on now? Who has the skills, ability, power and energy to get the result we want?
2.	Fact-Finding	Here's what we know. What don't we know? What do we need to know? Where could we possibly find the information? Get points of view from all involved, from the CEO to hourly employee.	Here's what we've found. What's relevant to our situation? What's irrelevant?
3.	Problem Definition	What are the key facts? Generate a list of challenge statements. Ask: 'How might we ... ? What if ... ?'	Select a statement that best defines your problem.
4.	Idea Generation	List as many ideas and solutions as you can think of for resolving the problem or meeting the challenge. Don't evaluate or judge ideas. Piggyback or build on ideas of others to generate more ideas.	Narrow down the list to the four or five best ideas.
5.	Action Plan	Make a list of as many action steps as necessary to achieve your objective.	Put the steps in order and specify a date for each step to be completed.
6.	Evaluate	List criteria for evaluating options.	Evaluate each option against criteria.

Example

Henry is a sales manager who was experiencing problems with his sales reps not filling in their order forms properly. As a consequence, customers were being shipped the wrong orders. He used 'convergent' thinking to turn on his judgement and critical eye until he pinpointed the specific problems.

Henry then used 'divergent' thinking and evaluated what further problems this was causing, as well as how many sales reps weren't completely filling in the forms. He generated a list of ideas to get the sales reps to fill in all the blanks in the form.

He then switched back to 'convergent' thinking by analysing the various alternatives, then decided to create a simpler form. He also decided to train each sales rep to use the new form within a period of three weeks.

24. CHART ACTIONS

What It Is

A technique to document actions as they are discussed in a meeting and to record the specific actions to be taken after the meeting.

What You'll Need
- Flip chart
- Markers

How It Works

Create an 'Actions' chart with three columns. Title the columns 'What,' 'Who' and 'By When'.

List the ideas for action in the 'What' category as they come up in the meeting.

As team members discuss the ideas further, write down 'Who' will do what and 'By When'.

If the actions are not clear, wait until the end of the meeting to clarify these actions so as not to interrupt the flow of the meeting.

When all ideas have been discussed, wrap up your meeting by going back to the chart and confirming 'what' actions will be taken by 'who' and 'by when'.

	ACTIONS	
What	**Who**	**By When**

As a follow-up, be sure to have a list of these actions as one of your agenda items at the beginning of the next meeting.

25. PASSING NOTES

What It Is

A technique used for better communication among specific work groups or departments that are dependent upon one another to get their work done.

What You'll Need
- Stopwatch or timer
- Flip chart
- Notepaper
- Markers

How It Works

Team leader or facilitator explains that each person is a member of a team and teams must be dependent upon one another to be successful. The information derived from this exercise will be used to make plans to help support one another better and get work done.

Break team members into their specific work groups. Each group will write a note to the group upon which it depends. This note will begin with a phrase like:

'In order for us to meet our goals, we need you to …'

or

'In order for us to work more effectively, we need you to …' Be sure to make your request specific.

State the rationale for your request.

State how you will measure the results.

Honour others. No personal attacks are allowed.

When the notes are finished, ask each group to distribute its notes.

Ask each team to read all of its notes and formulate any questions for clarification.

A team may ask for clarification from another team by sending a team representative to the other team with the note to get clarification. Rebuttals or excuses are not allowed. Just listen.

Team representatives report what they learned.

When finished, teams are to start problem solving the issues expressed in their notes. This will result in a list of corrective actions to which they can commit.

Each team will pick a recorder, a reporter and a timekeeper.

Respond to each note or issue, one at a time. Brainstorm, if necessary.

Agree on corrective actions and document on charts. Include a contact or coordinator name for each action.

Ask each team to report the action plans for all the notes it received.

The teams that sent the notes then respond to the action plans with thumbs-up (affirm) or thumbs-down (deny) signals. The teams giving thumbs-down signals must briefly explain why they don't accept the action plans.

Ask teams to plan another meeting to work on issues left unresolved among themselves and other teams. This should be done immediately.

Plan a follow-up session or progress report including a specific date and time.

26. SWOT ANALYSIS

What It Is
A strategic planning tool for gathering information to be used in marketing, planning, strength building, goal setting and opportunity searching. SWOT stands for Strengths, Weaknesses, Opportunities and Threats. SWOT information provides a way for you to accurately determine your team's current performance, as well as provide a foundation for effectively and intelligently setting goals and priorities and making key decisions for the group's future.

Strengths and Weaknesses examine the internal environment of the group such as team-member skills, technology, communications, creativity and functions of the department. Opportunities and Threats focus on the external environment such as industry trends; competitors; and political, economic and social information.

What You'll Need
- Flip chart
- Markers

How It Works
All stakeholders should be asked to participate in SWOT Analysis. Ask the following four open-ended questions.
- What are our internal Strengths?
- What are our internal Weaknesses?
- What are our external Opportunities?
- What are our external Threats?

If you have a large group, divide participants into teams to analyse each of the four categories. Otherwise, conduct the SWOT Analysis as a group activity.

Give the teams specific exercise instructions, eg, time allowed to discuss each of the points. Pick a recorder, reporter and a timekeeper. Allow enough time for: 1. brainstorming process (30 minutes), 2. report back (5 minutes per group), and 3. evaluation (20 minutes) for subsequent planning for using this information.

On completion of the initial SWOT brainstorming session, each team reports team results to other teams.

Once the reporting has taken place, a new list is created from the combined information received. As a group, review the results of your SWOT Analysis.

Strengths	**Weaknesses**
Opportunities	**Threats**

Discuss: What are your reactions to the results of our SWOT Analysis? What in particular stands out for you? What did you find surprising/not surprising? What should we do with this information?

Finally, summarise the group's discussion and subsequent plans for using this information. Set timelines/actions to make changes and improvements.

Option

Prior to your SWOT Analysis meeting, additional information can be gathered in a number of ways: face-to-face interviews, questionnaires, e-mail and customer comment cards. Information on Opportunities and Threats can also be obtained from journals, magazines, newsletters, trade shows, conventions, federal reports, private research groups, and any other source pertinent to your organisation.

27. REPORTERS AND COLUMNISTS

What It Is
A monthly written communication for sharing information and ideas.

How It Works
Ask team members to write for your monthly newsletter. Getting your team members involved in contributing to a monthly communication is beneficial to opening the lines of communication. Contributions can include the following:
- Tips for doing a better job
- Heroes and heroines in the workplace
- Columns on the most exciting place they've ever visited
- The most dangerous thing they've ever done
- A celebrity they would like to meet and what they would ask that person
- A 'what's happening in team members' lives' column
- Reviews of movies and restaurants by team members
- Crossword puzzles with employees' names
- Jokes or humorous stories
- Inspirational story – 'Thought for the Month'
- The most important lesson they ever learned

Involve your team further by asking team members for other ideas for both content and design.

28. OPPOSITE THINKING

What It Is

Looking at possibilities by reversing your perspective in two ways:

1. By thinking in opposites, you'll discover things you normally miss. For instance, what is the opposite of what you're dealing with? If you're dealing with customer service, think of customer disservice. Are you doing more with less? Think of doing less with more.

2. Whatever you want to do, think of what everybody else does and then try the opposite. For instance, sending a letter of complaint. Usually everyone writes a letter and mails it to the head office. Instead, make an appointment with the president of the company to voice your complaint.

What You'll Need
- Flip chart
- Markers

How It Works

Teach team members how to do a task by exaggerating how not to do the task. When presented with a ridiculously bad example, employees can learn both the 'how-to's' and the 'how-not-to's' of the job.

Draw a 'T' on a flip chart and write a reverse statement of the problem as your heading on the left-hand side. On the right-hand side, write the word 'Reverse' as your heading.

Begin the activity by asking your team members to list as many negative ideas as possible.

When this has been accomplished, address the negative comments one by one by asking your team members how they can reverse the situation.

Encourage your team members to be creative and have fun.

Discuss the ideas and how they can be utilised.

Example

How we can make our customers go away	Reverse
Be rude.	Be courteous.
Ignore them.	Make eye contact and listen.
Don't answer the phone.	Answer within three rings.
Place them on hold.	Ask the caller if she will wait.
Don't listen.	Make eye contact, follow the speaker and paraphrase.
Don't keep promises.	Overdeliver and underpromise.

29. SCAVENGER HUNTS

What It Is

A fact-finding, team-building activity that quickly enables teams to develop team identity and team effectiveness.

What You'll Need

• Instruction sheets
• List of objects to obtain

How It Works

Give the team instruction sheets (eg, any physical boundaries) and a specific time period for completing the task.

Provide them with a comprehensive list of objects you wish them to obtain. These items must be realistic and easy to find.

When the activity has been completed, ask questions. How did they organise themselves? What was the method chosen? Were they successful? Were there any problems? What would they do differently?

Scavenger hunts are being used in companies for several different reasons.

- **New-hire orientation:** Create a hunt that sends new employees around the workplace meeting important people in the company, meeting co-workers, finding where departments are located, and retrieving essential information about how the company functions.
- **Familiarise team members to new cities:** Have employees find client offices, prominent landmarks, the convention centre. To prove that they successfully found each 'item', have them bring back some proof.
- **Customer service hunts:** Have employees search for 'moments of truth' throughout your own organisation, 'moments' when a customer would make a judgement (good and/or bad) about your organisation.
- **Competition hunts:** Have employees visit your competitor's establishment as a customer and search for 'moments of truth'. To prove that they successfully accomplished this activity, have them bring back some proof.

30. SKITS

What It Is

A skit is a way to highlight company issues for the upcoming year, including corporate objectives. It can be used as a creative way to share information in a short amount of time. Skits can also be used to share job information with other departments or to get a point across in an interesting, memorable way. Skits can be used to establish a high level of cohesiveness in a work team.

How It Works

Team members must agree on the key points to be made in the skit, then plan the best way to reveal those points. Skits should neither be too short nor too long. A good length is five to ten minutes. Acting skills are not a prerequisite.

Skits can be serious or funny and should not demean another team member. The important thing to remember is to make sure that the point of the skit can be clearly understood.

The debriefing exercise should take place in small work teams and should not be done by the team that presented the skit. The time allowed for this should be at least 15 minutes for each skit.

Debriefing questions include the following:

- What were the key points you observed?
- Was there anything that needed clarification?
- What was your reaction?
- What can you do to carry out the objectives or diminish the frustrations portrayed in the skit?

Ask each work team to create an action plan based on the information contained in its debriefing summary, and set a date for follow-up to ensure the action has been taken. Allow at least 20 minutes for planning.

Option
If you want to let everyone know about changes in roles or responsibilities within a department, a talk-show format can be fun and informative at the same time.

31. 'IN THE ZONE' THINKING

What It Is
A powerful thinking method that can be used by individuals or teams for decision making, goal setting, problem solving and even conflict resolution. It is a powerful method of getting team members to look at things from different perspectives. Using five colours to represent thinking directions, you will be able to generate new ideas as well as possible solutions.

What You'll Need
A set of colour indicators for each participant

How It Works
This activity gets team members to focus on the goal or issue at hand and to stay away from the past or what has been done.

The team leader posts the goal, problem or issue to be addressed and then begins the activity by saying 'Let's think in (colour) about the goal, problem or issue.'

Each member then inputs all thoughts and ideas represented by the colour.

Colour Indicators

Beige: Neutral (facts, figures, data, information)

Red: Dangers (suggest stopping, seriousness, carefulness, caution, weaknesses, emotions)

Yellow: Optimistic and positive (benefits, advantages, new ideas, possibilities, alternatives)

Green: Financial aspects (growth aspects, opportunities, implications, budget constraints)

Purple: Loyalty, order and direction (concerns with control and proper use of the colour zones)

Team members must stay in the colour zone until the team leader says, 'It is now time to address this issue from the (another colour) zone' or 'Let's move on to the (another colour) zone.'

All team members switch their thinking direction to the new colour zone. All team members stay in the same colour-zone thinking at all times. It is not necessary to go in a specific order and you can go back to a zone if the need arises. All team members must go back if the zone is changed back.

Suggested Meeting Agenda Planning

At the beginning

Beige zone: The reason for the meeting

The statement of the problem and desired outcome

A plan for sequence of 'zones' to be explored

At the end of the meeting

Beige zone: What has been achieved?

What is the design?

What is the solution?

What are the next steps?
Who will act on them?
By what time parameters?

32. FORTUNE COOKIES

What It Is

A creative discussion technique for team members to share information and their points of view.

What You'll Need

- Custom-made fortune cookies
- Off-the-shelf fortune cookies
- Refreshments

How It Works

Have your local bakery make fortune cookies with your own fortunes baked into them. These fortunes can be any issues you want the entire staff to address. Serve refreshments and these fortune cookies at one of your planning meetings. Have each team member share her fortune statement with the group. Allow enough time for team members to discuss these fortune statements and their ideas to solve complex issues.

Option

Off-the-shelf fortune cookies are also a way to open a meeting by having team members discuss their generic fortune statements, which have no bearing in particular other than to encourage communication. Allow one minute for each team member, then proceed with the formal portion of your meeting.

33. 'WHAT IF' THINKING

What It Is

A technique to loosen up your thinking by engaging your imagination in finding new ways of looking at how to do things.

What You'll Need

Flip chart to record responses

How It Works

To use it, choose a forthcoming task or a problem you have to solve and ask, 'What if?'

Have the group write down the answer in a period of one to two minutes, and then ask another 'what if' and so on.

Examples

Improve market share

'What if' _____

'What if' _____

'What if' _____

'What if' _____

'What if' _____

Market changes

'What if' _____

'What if' _____

'What if' _____

'What if' _____

'What if' _____

Cutting costs
    'What if' _____
    'What if' _____
    'What if' _____
    'What if' _____
    'What if' _____

34. EGG DROP

What It Is

A problem-solving, team-building activity

What You'll Need

- Timer and stopwatch
- 12 straws per team
- Masking tape
- Eggs (raw)
- Plastic sheets
- Ladder

How It Works

To demonstrate creativity through teamwork, divide your group into teams of eight. Give each team 12 straws, four strips of masking tape and a raw egg. The objective is for each team to manufacture a device in seven minutes that will keep the egg intact when it is dropped from a height of 10 feet.

Cover the floor area with plastic where the eggs are to be dropped. Adjust the ladder over that area. Each team will then test its invention.

After each team completes its experiment, the entire group listens to each team share how it devised its invention.

Team success depends on the dynamics: how creative the team was, whose ideas the team members were willing to accept, how they were able to identify and tap into a member's expertise or ideas.

The most important lesson to be learned is that the teams can be creative within time constraints.

35. MOVIE BREAKS

What It Is
A team-building activity

What You'll Need
- VCR
- TV
- Movies
- Refreshments

How It Works
Have the entire team watch a movie together and then have a snack afterwards and discuss the lessons of the movie. Successful examples of team building, problem solving, leadership, communication skills and dealing with difficult people can all be found in the following movies:
- 'Apollo 13'
- '12 Angry Men'
- 'To Sir, With Love'
- 'Mr Holland's Opus'

They're movies that illustrate a point. There are many others.

36. PROCESS FLOWCHART

What It Is

A technique used when you need to analyse a process or problem that involves many steps and many people. It is also used when you need to save time, money and resources, or improve efficiency. The team looks at all the steps in an existing series of progressive and interdependent steps to achieve an end result, and then looks for methods to improve that process.

What You'll Need

- Flip chart
- Post-it Notes
- Markers

How It Works

As a team, list all the steps involved from the beginning to the end of a process. Use Post-it Notes for each step in the process so you can move things around if needed. Place the Post-it Notes on a large piece of flip-chart paper on the wall.

When the process comes to a decision point, split your flowchart in many directions as options become available. Follow each new direction's process as well.

When finished with the current process, review the completed chart for possible gaps or inconsistencies.

With help from all involved, have the team analyse the current process and identify problems, unnecessary steps, and methods for measuring improvement.

Brainstorm and agree on changes to improve the process. Create a new process flowchart as a tool for documenting these changes.

Plan how to communicate the changes to others involved in the process, and schedule a specific follow-up time.

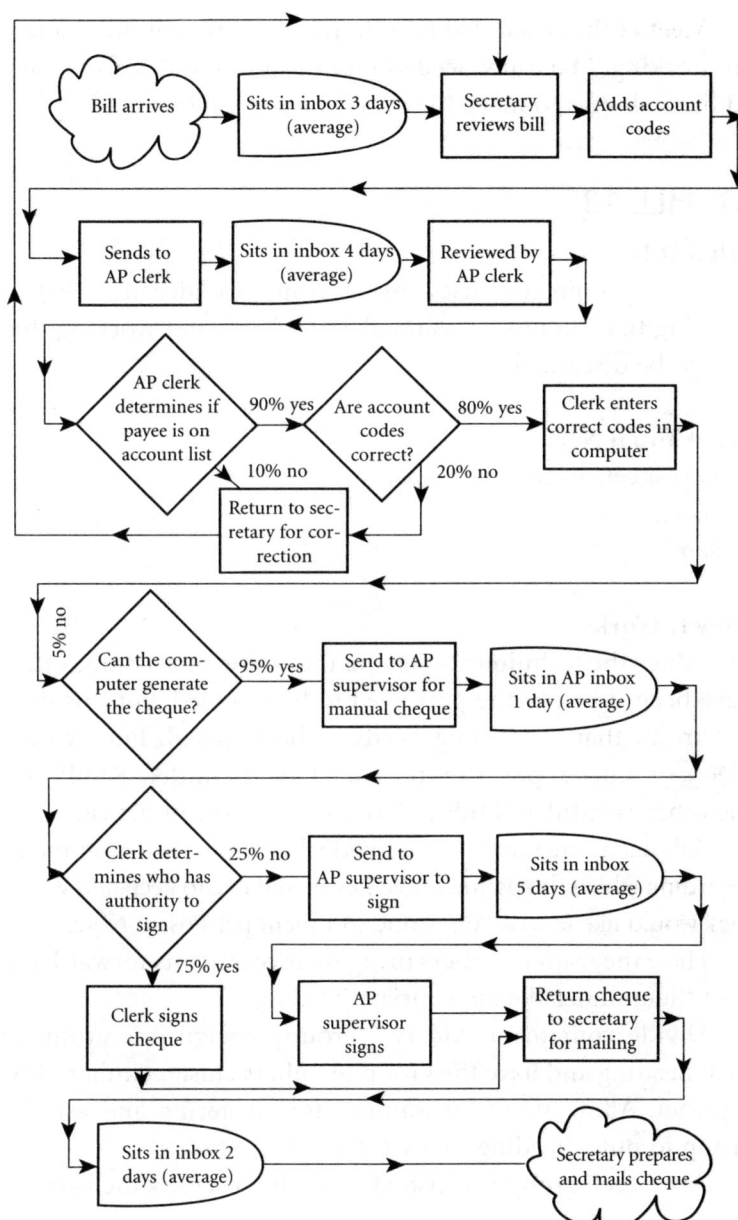

Bill arrives → Sits in inbox 3 days (average) → Secretary reviews bill → Adds account codes

Sends to AP clerk → Sits in inbox 4 days (average) → Reviewed by AP clerk

AP clerk determines if payee is on account list → 90% yes → Are account codes correct? → 80% yes → Clerk enters correct codes in computer

10% no

20% no

Return to secretary for correction

5% no

Can the computer generate the cheque? → 95% yes → Send to AP supervisor for manual cheque → Sits in AP inbox 1 day (average)

Clerk determines who has authority to sign → 25% no → Send to AP supervisor to sign → Sits in inbox 5 days (average)

75% yes

Clerk signs cheque

AP supervisor signs → Return cheque to secretary for mailing

Sits in inbox 2 days (average) → Secretary prepares and mails cheque

Meet at the scheduled time to review how well the changes are working. Make any needed modifications and consider any additional ways to make the process more effective.

37. FILE 13

What It Is
File 13 is a process used by a group to identify what is working that should be retained and what is not working that should be discarded.

What You'll Need
- Two sheets of butcher paper
- Post-it Notes
- Pens

How It Works
Introduce the technique by saying that some of the things they have been doing in the past need to be changed, but this does not mean that everything needs to be changed. Put two big pieces of butcher paper on the wall. One is entitled 'KEEP,' and the other is entitled 'FILE 13,' meaning 'to toss or get rid of'.

Ask team members to individually write their comments regarding which things/methods they would like to keep and which they would like to toss. Allow one comment per Post-it Note.

Have the team members bring their comments forward and post them under the appropriate heading.

Divide your team into two groups. Assign one group to each heading and have the group members cluster similar ideas together. Allow about 10 minutes for clustering and ask the group to put a heading on each cluster.

After each group is finished, have them review the work of

the other group. When they have read all of the clusters in both categories, ask them to sit down for a debriefing.

Debrief the exercise by discussing reactions, conclusions and what should be done with the information.

Incorporate the information as the team suggests, keeping what needs to be kept and tossing what can be discarded into File 13.

38. WORKING BREAKS

What It Is
A working break is a short, informal time specifically set aside within the time frame of a meeting to take care of addressing one-on-one issues without wasting the time of other meeting participants.

What You'll Need
List of ground rules

How It Works
Create a specific time on your meeting agenda that allows for individual team members or small groups to take care of private business that isn't related to your scheduled agenda items.

Until your group is familiar with the purpose and procedures of working breaks, bring a prepared Ground Rules Chart with you and post it in a conspicuous place. Be sure to call attention to the ground rules before taking the working breaks.

Example: Working Break Ground Rules
Discuss only issues that are one-on-one or small-group issues. Anything relevant to the entire group must be discussed on the regular agenda.

Make it short. Use this time to make appointments or to check suppliers, deadlines, etc.

Stay in the room, but stand up and move around.

If the person you wish to talk with is engaged, stand nearby to indicate that you are waiting.

If you have no business to attend to with anyone else, stay available for others who might have business with you.

39. LEARNING LOG

What It Is

A tool to encourage team members to make learning a habit.

What You'll Need

A spiral notebook or empty journal for each participant

How It Works

Encourage each team member to keep a learning log!

Have them write down interesting things they learn from books, other people, observations, the Web, etc. Set aside a specific time each month to ask them to share some of the items from their logs.

Ask them if there are any ideas they have logged that might be implemented to improve service, quality, processes, systems and products to the end user in your place of business or organisation.

Creating a specific time for your team members to share what they have learned will translate into the enhancement of skills essential to achieving results.

40. TELL STORIES

What It Is

A creative tool to stimulate imagination and thinking processes to find solutions and better ways of doing things.

What You'll Need

Stories that you have read, experienced yourself, or observed through the experiences of others that have meaningful messages for you

How It Works

Learning to tell stories in an interesting manner enhances creativity of both the teller and the listener. Stories illustrate behaviour in ways that take listeners away from their current situations and let them learn about similar situations. This allows listeners to draw lessons from the stories that they can apply to their own situations.

Use stories in your meetings to effectively demonstrate a point that will inspire participants to take action. Using a variety of stories will eliminate the sameness and/or routines of each meeting.

The previous chapters in this book are filled with wonderful stories that make great points.

Here's an example of such a story.

There's a potent and very useful lesson to learn in an old Chinese story. The Emperor had heard many glowing tales about an aged couple who lived deep in the country. It was amazing that the old couple had celebrated their 80th wedding anniversary.

What was even more extraordinary was the fact that the couple was reputed never to have had a serious quarrel. They had raised many children, who lived very close to home, with no family squabbles. The Emperor summoned the old man from afar and had him sit in a room all alone at a table with paper, pen and ink.

The Emperor ordered the old man to start writing: 'I want you to write the secret of your wondrously successful marriage and family life.' The old man picked up the pen and immediately started writing. When the Emperor returned hours later, the old man was still writing. At once he put down the pen and handed over the many sheets of paper. On each sheet, the old man had written hundreds of times just one word, 'Patience!'

Explain why you use a story to make a point.

41. CAUSE-AND-EFFECT DIAGRAM

What It Is

A cause-and-effect diagram such as the Ishikawa Fishbone is used to determine possible causes by identifying effects in several categories. Analysing the problem with this thinking tool will help team members identify specific reasons.

What You'll Need
- Flip chart
- Markers

How It Works

Present team members with a statement of the problem.

Have team members write down the problem characteristics.

Example

Bad coffee is the problem.

List all the possible reasons why the coffee may be the problem in the six categories of problem characteristics listed on the chart below.

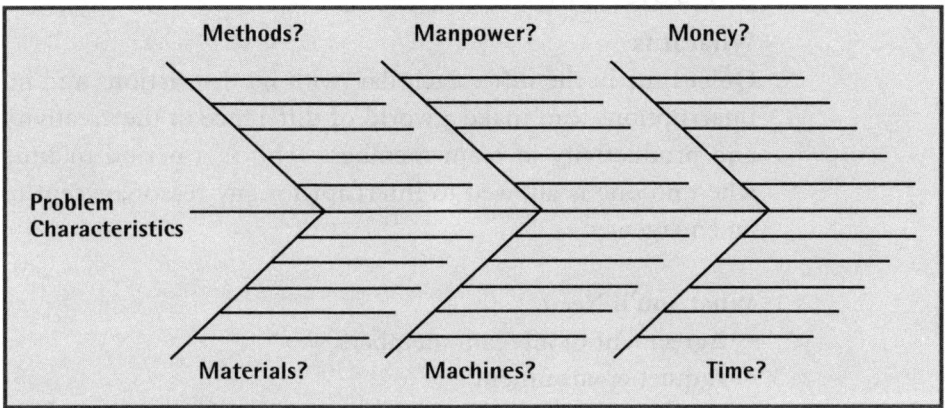

42. THINKING BACKWARDS

What It Is

A technique to think differently, especially when team members are experiencing frustrations in their jobs.

How It Works

Have your team identify a desired outcome by stating specifically what the problem is. Then, start at the desired outcome and work backwards step by step, answering the following questions:

- 'In order for this step to be accomplished, what has to happen before it?'
- 'What would the timeline be to do this step?'

Ask the same questions over and over until you get to a starting point.

Thinking backwards very often eliminates mistakes that otherwise would have been missed by more common thought processes.

43. QUIET TIME

What It Is

Quiet time in the office each day, with no distractions and no interruptions, can make a world of difference in the creativity and productivity of team members. This is a period of time when no one is allowed to interrupt for any reason, except in an emergency.

What You'll Need

- Agreement of all team members
- A quiet environment

How It Works

Make a commitment to spend at least five to 15 minutes per day in silence, to have a break from any activity and to refresh and invigorate. Many of the greatest geniuses have made this a practice. Many breakthrough ideas have occurred while daydreaming!

Option

Meditation is the practice of developing self-knowledge and inner peace through deep relaxation and reflection. Meditation is a time to sit quietly with eyes closed while the mind is emptied of all persistent thoughts, worries or concerns.

Try performing a simple meditation by selecting a number between one and 10. Breathe in, think of the number you selected, breathe out, breathe in, think of the number you selected, breathe out. Continue doing this for a period of five minutes.

Minds that are constantly filled with everyday problems and irritations need to be refreshed with positive thoughts. Try cleansing your mind through meditation by using various colours. Red represents strength and vitality (when you need persistence); green represents healing and harmony (when you want to feel greater love for others); blue represents peace and serenity (when you need to relax); yellow represents happiness (when you want to attract others); purple represents creativity (when you want to be more creative).

As with any form of meditation, begin by making yourself comfortable, close your eyes and select one of the colours, then visualise the colour and its qualities. Let the colour wash through your body from the top of your head to the tips of your toes. Do this for no less than seven minutes. When you have finished, silently affirm to yourself the qualities of the colour and their effect on you.

44. OPTIONS CRITERIA WORKSHEET

What It Is

An options criteria worksheet is a technique designed to prioritise a group of potential alternatives under consideration. This is a tool to help you quickly 'see' what might be the best option.

What You'll Need

Worksheets

How It Works

Prepare worksheets, which should comprise charts with columns. List the necessary criteria across the top. Use as many or as few columns as you need. Criteria are used to rate and select the best options and must be written in the same form.

List the potential options down the left side of the page.

Do the exercise by going down each column, using a rating scale. Rate all options, one criterion at a time. Complete the column for one criterion before moving to the next column.

You may use any rating scale that works for you. Example: 5 = Excellent, 4 = Very Good, 3 = Good, 2 = OK, 1 = Poor.

After filling in all the boxes, total the scores for each option.

Example: The Options Criteria Worksheet – Hiring a New Assistant

CRITERIA					
Options	Typing	Public Relations	Design Exp.	Budgeting	Total
Susan	5	3	2	1	11
Jim	4	5	4	5	18
Bill	3	2	5	3	13
Mary	1	4	5	5	15
Tom	4	5	5	5	19

45. OTHER PERSON'S SHOES

What It Is

A technique to ensure that all team members listen, understand, and can explain the perspectives being presented in a meeting.

What You'll Need

List of ground rules

How It Works

Post the ground rules and be sure to explain them so that everyone understands what is expected.

Introduce this exercise during a part of the meeting when it is important that the opinions of all team members are understood.

Ask participants, whenever they speak or voice an opinion, to first repeat what they understood the previous team member to have said, including facts and feelings. This does not mean that they agree with the other team member, simply that they understand.

After the summary, ask the team member whose viewpoint was being summarised to confirm that she was heard correctly. If needed, the team leader or facilitator can ask questions for clarification.

Continue working through the agenda.

When offering solutions, team members should offer solutions that would be acceptable if they were in the other person's shoes.

Example: Ground Rules for Other Person's Shoes

Before speaking, repeat what you understood the last team member to have said. Look at the team member whose perspective you are summarising.

Be sure to include facts and feelings that the other team member might have.

Use supportive vocal intonations and respect the other person's perspective. Sarcasm is not acceptable. Put yourself in the other person's shoes.

46. MASH DECISION MAKING

What It Is

This is a technique for making quick decisions in critical situations. 'MASH' (which stands for mobile army surgical hospital) was the longest running situation comedy on television. The show was set during the Korean War in a medical unit and starred Alan Alda, Gary Burghoff and Loretta Swit. During emergencies, decisiveness was a critical component of survival. The MASH decision-making technique was based on placing the wounded into three categories:

1. Those who would die, no matter what was done.
2. Those who would survive, even if nothing was done right away.
3. Those who were in between where immediate attention would save them.

How It Works

Ask your team members to list six of their most important priorities.

Ask them if any of their priorities are probably going to die despite the application of enormous efforts. (Those who would die, no matter what was done.)

Ask them if there are any activities that will survive even if they never do another thing personally. (Those who would survive, even if nothing was done right away.)

Their remaining projects and priorities are the ones that need immediate attention to have a positive result. (Those who were in between where immediate attention would save them.)

Each team member must then make a list of what needs to be done for each priority and/or project. Are there any concerns or obstacles? What actions need to be taken? What are the timelines?

Categorising priorities and projects will give a whole new perspective and sense of order.

Priority/Project	Concerns/Obstacles	Actions to Be Taken	By When

47. PNP THINKING

What It Is

A powerful thinking tool that will enable you to deliberately direct your attention first towards the Positive points, then towards the Negative points and finally towards the Possibility points. When used deliberately and in a disciplined manner, this exercise will accomplish an extensive exploration of an idea.

What You'll Need
- Flip chart
- Markers

How It Works

A **PNP** can be done in three minutes. You can use the PNP in one of two ways: either on your own or in a small discussion group with your team members.

P stands for the Positives.

N stands for the Negatives.

P stands for the Possibilities.

Example: Do a PNP on the reasons why schedules should be changed to flextime.

POSITIVES	NEGATIVES	POSSIBILITIES
Cover more hours	Harder to schedule	Different combinations of teams
Happier employees	Resistance to change	Who would support it
Productivity increase	Lack of continuity for customer contact	Reduction in personal phone calls
Reduced employee complaints	Harder to maintain quality control	Customer service improves

Doing this exercise is fairly easy. What might be difficult is letting go of any prejudices you may have when you are forced to direct your attention deliberately in one direction and then another. Once you're forced to think in other ways, then the challenge is to find as many **P** or **N** or **P** points as possible. This tool allows the thinker to look outside the normal judgemental framework of good or bad. When the **PNP** method is used, people find that their emotions are applied after the exploration in decision making versus their emotions being applied before and preventing exploration. They usually find that their feelings about the subject matter change from what they felt at the outset.

48. PANEL OF EXPERTS

What It Is

An imaginary board of powerful business leaders and innovators who will support and advise you in surmounting business challenges. The people you select are people you know personally or who have a celebrity status of one kind or another. Imagine having Albert Einstein, John F Kennedy, Lee Iacocca, Henry Ford, Andrew Carnegie, Margaret Thatcher, Mother Teresa,

Bill Gates, Thomas Edison, Nelson Mandela, Sam Walton or any other person (family members or friends are optional) on your board. The people on your panel of experts can either be living or dead, well-known or unknown. Discuss how these people would solve a problem you have or would find innovative ideas and applicable solutions to your current situation.

What You'll Need
- Flip chart
- Markers

How It Works
Ask your team members to select two to four people, living or dead, whom they most admire.

Then ask them to write down one or two traits or qualities that they most admire about these people.

Once they have done this, have them write down what made these people stand out and what was the feat for which they will be most remembered.

Take a challenge or problem you have at the current time. Ask your team members to consult their panel of experts to imagine how they would solve it. Example: How would Sam Walton resolve a pilferage problem? In what ways would Albert Einstein look for new solutions? How would Nelson Mandela resolve a labour dispute?

Allow each team member five minutes to discuss their ideas. Record all ideas for further evaluation relative to the current business issue or challenge.

Option
Encourage your team members to research their most admired people. Have them find information that gives further insight

into how they became so successful. Ask them to take notes on anything that elaborates what their abilities were/are and how they overcame obstacles.

49. GUIDED VISUALISATION

What It Is

An effective method for tapping into thinking processes to gain access to experiences, images, ideas, facts and knowledge that are stored in the brain. Very often this knowledge is difficult to access in a conscious state of mind. Visualisation can cultivate relaxation in order to allow this stored information to flow into one's awareness.

How It Works

Choose something to visualise about. It may be a statement of a problem, a work situation, an opportunity for improvement or a process. Create mental pictures of the problem you are trying to solve.

Questions you can ask to stimulate thinking could include the following:

- What change would you like to have?
- What does it look like?
- Who would do what best?
- How would you illustrate or describe a perfect situation?
- Where would the solution come from?
- What could you improve?

Ask your team members to close their eyes and relax by having them imagine themselves in a favourite place. Ask them to let their minds wander and be open and alert to any images or words that come to mind. Allow at least five minutes.

Have them record any ideas that surface even if they are incomplete. Discuss all ideas to see if they produce any other thoughts.

Select the ideas that the team believes to have the most potential for further exploration. If necessary, the team can come back to any of these ideas at a later date.

Option
Ask your participants to stand and to spread out far enough so that when their arms are extended they will touch no one.

Tell them to raise their right arms in front of them and turn their bodies to the right at the waist with their right arms still extended and to go as far around as they can. Have them mark the degree of rotation by finding a fixed point.

Now ask them to bring their arms back down to their sides. Then ask them to close their eyes and, without physically moving, visualise repeating the exercise in their minds to the point they marked, then to go three inches beyond the first point and find a second point. Finally have them visualise another three inches to a third point.

Now ask them to open their eyes. Guide them through the rotation exercise again. Nearly everyone will go farther than they did the first time.

Have them discuss the power of visualisation, the importance of expectations, the effectiveness of focus and the value of goals.

50. CHANGE SIDES

What It Is
A method for gaining insight and perspective on the challenges you have by examining the opposition's point of view.

How It Works

Have your team members imagine that everything about their current situation is the same, except that they are now the competitor.

Team members must imagine that they have the strengths, weaknesses, opportunities and threats of their competitor.

The idea is to have your team members find ways to beat themselves. Ask them to consider the situation in these new circumstances.

What would they do? For example: What would be the strategy? What would be the first steps taken?

Once all relevant questions have been asked, determine what the counter strategies would be. Then start accomplishing them.

51. RECORDING IDEAS

What It Is

A way to record ideas right away. So many ideas are lost because they are not written down at the precise time that they are thought of. Capturing a few of the thoughts you have every day will eventually lead to more and more useful, realistic ideas and solutions that work.

What You'll Need

Any of the following will do:
- Notebook
- Tape recorder
- Blank paper
- Customised thinking forms

How It Works

The intention of recording ideas is to record the idea as you think of it. Record all ideas, even the bad or incomplete ones.

A notebook is perfect for writing down any new and incomplete ideas. A notebook allows for easy review.

A tape recorder is always useful when it's not convenient to write. You may never use the ideas you record, but the act of recording stimulates more ideas.

Blank paper allows you to scribble or draw any word or image that comes to mind. Ideas come to us when we least expect them (for example, in the middle of the night)! Having paper readily available is smart.

Thinking forms are customised to your needs and what you wish to capture.

Idea	Reason Why it Will Work	Reason Why It Won't Work

52. WHAT'S ON YOUR MIND?

What It Is

This is an effective tool to help your team members share their ideas for continuous improvement and self-renewal.

What You'll Need

Customised forms with your company logo

How It Works .

Formally introduce your new idea-form and explain its purpose to all team members. What is its focus, its mission and its benefits?

Once the idea has been received, follow through with feedback.

See example below.

WHAT'S ON YOUR MIND?

See a situation that needs attention? Got an idea? Share it!

You do not have to write your name. Your suggestions and solutions will be commented upon by a manager or director from the appropriate department. Comments will be posted in the associate break room or written in the newsletter.

| NAME | DEPARTMENT | DATE |

The situation or problem as I see it is:

My suggestion for improving or solving it is:

BIBLIOGRAPHY

Adams, James L. *Conceptual Blockbusting: A Guide to Better Ideas.* New York: W.H. Freeman & Co, 1989.

Baker, Sam S. *Your Key to Creative Thinking.* New York: Harper & Row Publishers, 1962.

Bandler, Richard. *Using Your Brain for a Change.* Utah: Real People Press, 1985.

Barker, Joel A. *Paradigms: The Business of Discovering the Future.* New York: Harper, 1993.

Buzan, Tony. *Use Both Sides of Your Brain.* New York: Penguin Group, 1991.

—*Make the Most of Your Mind.* New York: Linden Press, 1984.

de Bono, Edward. *Lateral Thinking: Creativity Step by Step.* New York: Harper & Row, 1970.

Edelston, Martin and Marion Buhagiar. *'I' Power: The Secrets of Great Business in Bad Times.* Greenwich, CT: Boardroom Books, 1992.

Imai, Masaaki. *Kaizen: The Key to Japan's Competitive Success.* New York: Random House Business Division, 1986.

Lamberg, Lynne. *Bodyrhythms: Chronobiology and Peak Performance.* New York: William Morrow, 1994.

Maxwell, John C. *Developing the Leader Within You.* Tennessee: Thomas Nelson Inc., 1993.

Osborn, Alex. *Applied Imagination.* Buffalo: Creative Education Press, 1993.

VanGundy, Arthur B. *Idea Power: Techniques & Resources to Unleash the Creativity in Your Organisation.* New York: AMA-COM, 1992.

Wonder, Jacquelyn and Priscilla Donovan. *Whole-Brain Thinking: Working from Both Sides of the Brain to Achieve Peak Job Performance.* New York: Ballantine Books, 1984.

INDEX

Since 1993, Fiona Carmichael and Judi Moreo, as co-owners of Turning Point International Inc., have helped hundreds of organisations worldwide create 'thinking' cultures that improve leadership and managerial effectiveness, increase sales and empower individuals to achieve higher levels of performance and productivity.

Through keynote presentations, training, consulting and high impact learning resources like:

Ignite The Spark

they have built a solid reputation for getting positive results for client organisations of all types and sizes.

Contact Turning Point International at:
Tel: USA (702) 896-2228
Email: turningpoint21@att.net
Website: www.turningpointintl.com

Fiona Carmichael

In today's rapidly changing marketplace Fiona knows that people are a company's greatest asset and uses her strong business background to help people tap into their inner being to utilise their strengths and expand their skills. She understands the indispensable requirements for success and combines this with her ability to connect with the audience to achieve their goals with measurable and long-lasting results.

Using vivid descriptions and examples from her strong business experience and own personal triumphs, Fiona helps audiences realise that every person holds the roadmap to his or her own destiny. Fiona believes that every person has the power within and has untapped potential just waiting to be unleashed. In each of her presentations Fiona distils her knowledge and experience in a down to earth and convincing style to inform, encourage and build skills that can be implemented today for success tomorrow.

Fiona is the co-founder of Turning Point International, a human performance improvement company, originally established in South Africa which is now headquartered in Las Vegas, Nevada and has worked with hundreds of companies on three continents.

Judi Moreo

Judi Moreo has presented keynote speeches, workshops, and seminars in twenty-six countries on four continents.

Prior to becoming a full-time professional speaker, Judi was a successful entrepreneur. As owner of Universal Models, she became one of Las Vegas' most well known and respected businesswomen. The Las Vegas Chamber of Commerce honoured her as 'Woman of Achievement – Entrepreneur'.

She is the Past President of both the Greater Las Vegas Advertising Federation and the Las Vegas Professional Speakers Association, served as the Western Regional Adviser for the prestigious National Speakers Association for two years, and was awarded the 'Outstanding Achievement and Community Service Award' by the American Women in Radio and Television.

In 1994, Judi co-founded Turning Point International, an international performance improvement company, with headquarters in Las Vegas, Nevada. Turning Point International's services are in demand worldwide.